The Decision to Delist from the Stock Market

Barbara Fidanza • Ottorino Morresi
Alberto Pezzi

The Decision to Delist from the Stock Market

Theory and Empirical Evidence of Going Private

palgrave
macmillan

Barbara Fidanza
Department of Law
University of Macerata
Macerata, Italy

Ottorino Morresi
Department of Economics
Roma Tre University
Rome, Italy

Alberto Pezzi
Department of Business Studies
Roma Tre University
Rome, Italy

ISBN 978-3-030-06962-9 ISBN 978-3-319-95049-5 (eBook)
https://doi.org/10.1007/978-3-319-95049-5

Softcover re-print of the Hardcover 1st edition 2018

Cover credit: Brain light / Alamy Stock Photo
Cover design by AKIHIRO NAKAYAMA

This Palgrave Macmillan imprint is published by the registered company Springer Nature Switzerland AG
The registered company address is: Gewerbestrasse 11, 6330 Cham, Switzerland

Preface

Most books link a firm's decision to leave the stock market to the concept of buyout and analyze the causes and consequences of this corporate choice from the perspective of the buyer, the target firm, the combined entity that could result from the deal, and their shareholders. It is hardly surprising that books on buyouts are included in the merger and acquisition (M&A) literature. Delisting due to buyout is therefore merely considered an outcome of the deal and not the direct choice of the firm with its reasons and effects.

Delisting can be divided into involuntary and voluntary delisting. In the first case, the company is involuntarily forced to remove itself from the stock exchange due to non-compliance with regulatory requirements or because the company has gone into bankruptcy/liquidation. Voluntary delistings are, on the other hand, a consequence of a managerial choice and in this specific case, we refer to the concept of "going private transactions" (GPT) or "public-to-private" (PTP) operations. They lead to simultaneous delisting from all lists (domestic or otherwise) without subsequent trading. When companies are delisted from one market but continue to trade in another, the transaction is called "going dark" or "deregistration". It is not a real delisting but a form of delisting that describes a step down in the firm's quotation cycle because the firm starts trading in markets that are less regulated or not regulated at all. In this case, a change in corporate control is not necessary.

This book adopts a different approach and focuses its attention both on the voluntary and involuntary decision to remove the firm and its publicly traded shares from the stock market. This approach allows us to refocus the goal of the research work which no longer analyzes the transaction from the M&A market's point of view but examines the motives and effects of ending the firm's share trading. The buyout is therefore only viewed as a way of obtaining the termination of trading in the public market.

The book first provides some data on the geographical and historical importance of the phenomenon and compares it with the Initial Public Offering (IPO) market in order to show how it has increased and fluctuated over time and across different stock exchanges in response to market-wide factors. It then explains the most common techniques such as mergers, reverse stock splits, tender offers, and so on, that are used to delist a firm and the US regulation that disciplines the procedure for implementing them.

After clarifying the aim of the research work, the book provides the reader with a wide and systematic description of the theoretical approaches that are proposed in order to explain the choice such as information-based theories, access to capital, stock liquidity, corporate governance, listing requirements, short-termism, the use of derivatives, takeover defense, agency problems, and finally it focuses on going private in firms with highly concentrated ownership structures.

Although the firm can leave the stock market in many ways, a leveraged buyout (LBO) is undeniably the most common and probably the most important method for achieving delisting. The second chapter therefore concentrates on LBOs in terms of historical trends, characteristics, and motivations.

Some delisted firms do not cease to be traded on the public market but simply move from official regulated markets to either unregulated Over the Counter (OTC) markets or less regulated markets. Although the choice is partially motivated by the same reasons that drive delisting, the second chapter also highlights the specific factors that can trigger the choice, typically related to the difference between the market of origin and destination.

The third chapter reviews the empirical literature. There are essentially three streams of empirical literature on delisting. The first one studies, in voluntary delisting, the link between the decision to undertake the operation and the determinants in accordance with the different theoretical models. These determinants pertain, for example, to the firm's financial structure and performance characteristics, business characteristics, and stock liquidity. The other two literature streams highlight the reasons that lead to involuntary delisting and study the effects of delisting on firm value.

Except for company size, ex-ante performance, and company age, other variables do not show clear-cut results. Small firms, firms with poor ex-ante performance and young firms are more likely to go private. In terms of value effect, voluntary delisting increases shareholders' wealth, whereas involuntary delisting leads to value destruction.

In the final chapter we analyze the link between delisting operations and agency costs by using a sample of non-financial firms which voluntarily delisted from the London Stock Exchange main market between 2010 and 2016. We also analyze the relationship with other variables such as leverage or the number of years that a firm remains listed on the stock exchange.

University of Macerata, Macerata, Italy — Barbara Fidanza
Roma Tre University, Rome, Italy — Ottorino Morresi
Roma Tre University, Rome, Italy — Alberto Pezzi

Contents

List of Tables

CHAPTER 1

Facts, Figures and Theory

Ottorino Morresi

1.1 Introduction

The theoretical literature on the decision to go public is extensive and includes a large number of contributions that try to model how, when, and why a firm may decide to list its shares on a stock exchange. However, it has always been difficult to perform empirical studies that directly test for factors explaining why companies go public. This difficulty is typically related to data constraints. Significant efforts to overcome this issue were made, among others, by Rydqvist and Högholm (1995), Pagano et al. (1998), Brau and Fawcett (2006), Bancel and Mittoo (2009), Kim and Weisbach (2008) and Aslan and Kumar (2011) who have tried to empirically investigate the reasons for going public. The reverse process, that is, the process to remove a firm and its publicly traded shares from a market has not been empirically investigated much either even though this decision has become increasingly popular. Also in the case of delisting, the reasons why this choice has been poorly empirically investigated are mainly linked to data unavailability.

Table 1.1 clearly shows that since the 1990s the practice of delisting has spread over the major stock exchanges around the world, involving a significant and increasing number of firms. More interestingly, after 2000, the number of delisted firms often outnumbers the number of newly listed ones in the stock exchanges located in developed economies. Second, as can be expected, new listings tend to overcome delistings during periods of booming stock markets (2004–2007) while the opposite occurs during

B. Fidanza et al., *The Decision to Delist from the Stock Market*,
https://doi.org/10.1007/978-3-319-95049-5_1

Table 1.1 Newly listed and delisted firms around the world (1996–2017)

		1996	*1997*	*1998*	*1999*	*2000*	*2001*	*2002*	*2003*	*2004*	*2005*	*2006*	*2007*	*2008*	*2009*	*2010*	*2011*	*2012*	*2013*	*2014*	*2015*	*2016*	*2017*
North America																							
American Stock Exchange (AMEX)	Newly listed	97	104	100	90	112	44	43	76	89	97	70	92	NA	NA	NA	NA	NA	NA	NA	NA	NA	NA
	Delisted	137	80	NA	100	113	87	78	87	74	79	96	118	NA	NA	NA	NA	NA	NA	NA	NA	NA	NA
Mexico	Newly listed	11	22	3	3	2	4	6	78	110	12	31	63	43	42	27	63	NA	NA	3	8	4	5
	Delisted	9	14	6	8	15	9	9	10	9	6	22	32	37	9	2	17	18	2	2	2	3	1
Nasdaq	Newly listed	655	648	487	614	605	144	121	56	170	139	156	290	177	131	195	151	NA	NA	176	565	71	89
	Delisted	121	717	906	873	700	815	535	410	NA	NA	NA	348	289	302	269	249	261	180	182	197	244	NA
NYSE	Newly listed	278	273	205	151	122	144	151	107	152	146	118	126	71	99	163	144	NA	NA	179	111	76	131
	Delisted	100	171	194	254	286	215	145	111	107	135	138	232	155	212	154	141	114	151	99	148	181	NA
Toronto	Newly listed	168	193	116	144	113	84	NA	NA	NA	NA	NA	NA	NA	NA	NA	NA	NA	NA	NA	NA	NA	NA
	Delisted	103	96	103	121	151	181	NA	NA	NA	NA	NA	NA	NA	NA	NA	NA	NA	NA	NA	NA	NA	NA
TMX Group	Newly listed	NA	NA	NA	NA	NA	NA	194	204	346	388	383	408	359	207	333	369	NA	NA	67	116	30	96
	Delisted	NA	NA	NA	NA	NA	NA	367	345	291	215	212	249	296	383	278	230	175	262	202	199	213	204
South America																							
Lima	Newly listed	37	35	17	27	18	12	10	7	12	8	4	14	23	5	14	11	NA	NA	8	9	10	10
	Delisted	38	25	16	37	30	12	7	10	15	8	7	11	5	9	6	5	3	10	13	9	9	11
Sao Paulo (B3—Brasil Bolsa Balcão)	Newly listed	26	19	57	15	24	10	13	10	19	13	32	70	11	13	52	15	NA	NA	2	0	0	10
	Delisted	19	28	67	63	44	36	42	31	22	18	25	16	23	20	24	25	25	12	12	15	12	55
Europe																							
Amsterdam	Newly listed	9	16	23	23	NA	NA	NA	NA	NA	NA	NA	NA	NA	NA	NA	NA	NA	NA	NA	NA	NA	NA
	Delisted	12	12	NA	NA	NA	NA	NA	NA	NA	NA	NA	NA	NA	NA	NA	NA	NA	NA	NA	NA	NA	NA
Barcelona	Newly listed	8	35	75	129	101	115	NA	NA	NA	NA	NA	NA	NA	NA	NA	NA	NA	NA	NA	NA	NA	NA
	Delisted	14	16	20	21	18	9	NA	NA	NA	NA	NA	NA	NA	NA	NA	NA	NA	NA	NA	NA	NA	NA
BME Spanish Exchanges	Newly listed	NA	NA	NA	NA	NA	NA	514	275	NA	NA	NA	192	143	38	53	88	NA	NA	258	185	47	33
	Delisted	NA	NA	NA	NA	NA	NA	33	67	NA	NA	NA	NA	NA	NA	NA	145	116	80	49	39	192	402

Brussels	Newly listed	6	19	24	23	NA	NA	NA	NA	NA	NA	NA	NA	NA	NA	NA	NA	NA	NA	NA	NA	NA	NA
	Delisted	13	23	21	25	NA	NA	NA	NA	NA	NA	NA	NA	NA	NA	NA	NA	NA	NA	NA	NA	NA	NA
Copenhagen	Newly listed	8	5	11	6	8	5	0	2	3	NA	NA	NA	NA	NA	NA	NA	NA	NA	NA	NA	NA	NA
	Delisted	11	6	8	18	15	23	16	9	12	NA	NA	NA	NA	NA	NA	NA	NA	NA	NA	NA	NA	NA
Deutsche	Newly listed	403	765	67	168	152	21	6	0	6	15	35	65	189	29	108	216	NA	NA	16	25	19	16
Börse	Delisted	NA	NA	NA	NA	NA	NA	NA	NA	NA	NA	NA	40	44	61	45	32	51	37	68	70	45	29
Euronext	Newly listed	NA	NA	NA	NA	106	49	18	24	32	34	52	92	36	14	52	45	NA	NA	35	58	28	26
	Delisted	NA	NA	NA	NA	80	140	99	82	67	65	54	100	66	46	55	60	64	48	47	44	45	50
Helsinki	Newly listed	3	12	12	28	20	9	3	1	1	NA	NA	NA	NA	NA	NA	NA	NA	NA	NA	NA	NA	NA
	Delisted	9	1	7	8	12	12	9	5	9	NA	NA	NA	NA	NA	NA	NA	NA	NA	NA	NA	NA	NA
Milan Stock	Newly listed	15	13	22	36	49	18	14	11	10	19	45	33	9	8	2	3	2	7	6	10	7	10
Exchange (Borsa Italiana)	Delisted	21	22	18	9	22	21	13	27	11	15	17	16	16	12	10	12	9	13	11	13	10	8
London Stock	Newly listed	397	254	202	187	399	245	228	201	423	626	576	411	185	73	174	NA	110	143	189	142	115	163
Exchange (LSE)	Delisted	320	235	292	336	299	287	295	337	279	372	428	372	405	385	287	NA	204	167	205	213	200	166
Madrid	Newly listed	11	43	113	266	327	458	NA	NA	NA	NA	NA	NA	NA	NA	NA	NA	NA	NA	NA	NA	NA	NA
	Delisted	16	16	17	23	18	14	NA	NA	NA	NA	NA	NA	NA	NA	NA	NA	NA	NA	NA	NA	NA	NA
OMX (Nordic	Newly listed	NA	NA	NA	NA	NA	NA	NA	NA	NA	28	87	94	31	12	23	26	NA	NA	70	90	85	105
Exchanges)	Delisted	NA	NA	NA	NA	NA	NA	NA	NA	NA	36	53	33	62	39	42	38	40	30	38	31	40	NA
Oslo	Newly listed	23	56	29	10	25	17	6	5	22	46	33	58	15	3	19	13	NA	NA	19	11	7	17
	Delisted	16	11	11	30	26	19	15	30	12	15	22	25	15	26	17	17	13	21	17	17	11	11
Paris	Newly listed	65	86	240	73	NA	NA	NA	NA	NA	NA	NA	NA	NA	NA	NA	NA	NA	NA	NA	NA	NA	NA
	Delisted	72	59	67	72	NA	NA	NA	NA	NA	NA	NA	NA	NA	NA	NA	NA	NA	NA	NA	NA	NA	NA
Stockholm	Newly listed	18	54	36	54	46	24	10	4	10	NA	NA	NA	NA	NA	NA	NA	NA	NA	NA	NA	NA	NA
	Delisted	12	22	21	30	35	30	18	20	15	NA	NA	NA	NA	NA	NA	NA	NA	NA	NA	NA	NA	NA
Switzerland	Newly listed	7	13	17	19	28	21	6	2	4	11	9	10	7	2	1	0	NA	NA	0	3	3	4
	Delisted	20	21	20	32	24	25	20	23	14	NA	NA	NA	NA	NA	NA	11	12	NA	6	13	6	13

(*continued*)

Table 1.1 (continued)

		1996	*1997*	*1998*	*1999*	*2000*	*2001*	*2002*	*2003*	*2004*	*2005*	*2006*	*2007*	*2008*	*2009*	*2010*	*2011*	*2012*	*2013*	*2014*	*2015*	*2016*	*2017*
Asia-Pacific																							
Australia	Newly listed	75	87	63	128	175	80	89	107	186	232	NA	292	77	47	113	121	NA	NA	86	109	111	122
	Delisted	63	58	60	63	56	76	78	57	74	68	NA	104	65	93	87	112	96	95	76	75	129	70
Hong Kong	Newly listed	49	82	32	38	90	88	117	73	70	67	62	84	49	73	113	101	NA	NA	122	138	126	174
	Delisted	8	7	10	10	8	11	6	14	11	28	23	16	29	15	19	18	13	14	13	24	19	29
Korea	Newly listed	51	23	3	16	5	16	25	20	68	113	93	98	63	77	107	72	NA	NA	110	159	83	96
(Republic of)	Delisted	12	7	31	52	15	30	34	19	65	77	23	27	29	82	91	64	70	51	39	52	29	46
Shanghai	Newly listed	NA	NA	NA	NA	88	75	70	67	61	3	13	25	6	9	29	39	NA	NA	366	430	103	215
	Delisted	NA	NA	NA	NA	0	1	1	2	4	1	4	7	2	3	5	2	3	2	1	3	1	1
Singapore	Newly listed	24	41	23	53	87	37	32	60	82	68	67	76	43	25	36	24	NA	NA	32	15	19	24
	Delisted	2	3	8	12	15	25	24	10	10	8	19	18	28	20	36	34	19	28	30	14	30	27
Taiwan	Newly listed	36	26	35	33	80	70	86	47	38	13	11	30	31	36	41	48	NA	NA	17	18	25	21
	Delisted	1	4	2	8	11	16	31	14	10	19	14	20	12	3	12	8	6	7	7	8	10	8
Tokyo	Newly listed	61	51	57	75	206	93	94	120	153	99	114	68	54	23	26	50	NA	NA	92	110	96	104
	Delisted	19	19	32	30	45	48	82	67	53	54	49	70	79	78	68	52	56	65	42	67	68	41

Source: Our own elaborations with data from the World Federation of Exchanges, unless otherwise specified. LSE Group data between 2010 and 2017 come from LSE official historical statistics and include both the Main Market and the Alternative Investment Market (AIM). Milan Stock Exchange data between 2010 and 2017 come from Borsa Italiana official statistics and only include MTA (Main Market)

NA: Not available

Deutsche Börse: Since 1998 the number of companies does not include the market segment "Freiverkehr" (unofficial regulated market)

Euronext: Since 2000 Euronext has been managing the following stock exchanges: Paris, Amsterdam, Brussels, and Lisbon

TMX Group: The group was known as TSX Group and managed the Toronto Stock Exchange (TSX) and the Canadian Venture Exchange. Since 2007 it has also been managing the Montreal Stock Exchange that assumed the position of derivatives exchange in 1999 and was renamed TMX Group

BME: Since 2002 BME (Bolsas y Mercados Españoles) has been managing the following stock exchanges: Madrid, Barcelona, Bilbao, Valencia

OMX stock exchange was born in 2003 because of the merger between OM AB, that managed the Stockholm Stock Exchange, and the Helsinki Stock Exchange. As a result of a series of acquisitions, OMX has been managing the following stock exchanges: Stockholm, Helsinki, Tallinn, and Riga since 2003; Vilnius since 2004; Copenhagen since 2005; Iceland since 2006; Armenia since 2007. In 2007 OMX was acquired by the NASDAQ stock exchange

AMEX was acquired by the NYSE in 2008. The exchange was then integrated with the Alternext European small-cap exchange and renamed several times as NYSE Alternext US, NYSE AMEX Equities, NYSE MKT LLC, and finally NYSE American

LSE merged with Borsa Italiana (Italian Stock Exchange) in 2007 to form the LSE Group

falling stock markets (2001–2003 and 2008–2009). This behavior reflects the well-documented relevance of market timing factors based on the ability of managers to take advantage of favorable market conditions and the investor sentiment.[1] Third, stock exchanges in newly industrialized Asian economies appear to be less affected by this propensity toward delisting. In fact, the number of newly listed firms almost always exceeds the number of delisted ones regardless of the period investigated. However, this result is largely due to a marked increase in newly listed firms rather than a decrease in delisted firms. The number of delisted firms goes up over time in the same way as for stock exchanges in major advanced economies.

The picture depicted by these figures inspires some preliminary questions. Which factors may induce a firm to opt out of public markets? Which factors may reduce the attractiveness of having shares publicly traded on a stock market? Have these factors evolved over time? Does delisting occur in waves? Is it affected by clustering? What happens to delisted firms and their shares once they are removed from the stock market? Do all firms qualified as delisted firms really go private? Does delisting always mean going private? Before putting in order these questions, we need to define the term "delisting".

The broadest definition of delisting includes any share of a company that leaves the stock exchange on which it previously traded. The causes of delisting are quite numerous but can helpfully be distinguished according to criteria that take into account the theoretical foundations that the delisting is based on. Delisting can be classified depending on whether or not the firm leaves the stock exchange voluntarily. A firm may ***voluntarily*** leave the stock exchange for reasons such as mergers and acquisitions. ***Involuntary*** delisting may happen when a firm or its stocks fail to meet the listing requirements imposed by the exchange (e.g., the number of shareholders drops below a certain threshold, the firm goes bankrupt, the trading volume and/or market capitalization are insufficient, etc.). Sometimes a firm will voluntarily violate one of these listing standards in order to leave the

[1] The market timing argument is mainly developed within the IPO (Initial Public Offering) market (Ibbotson and Jaffe 1975; Ritter 1984; Lucas and McDonald 1990; Loughran et al. 1994; Pagano et al. 1998; Lowry 2003; Ritter and Welch 2002), but some empirical studies (Mitchell and Mulherin 1996; Brau et al. 2003) develop and find a similar regularity within takeovers that are one of the most important ways to delist a publicly traded firm. They find an increase in takeover activity during industry and economic downturns, and therefore, when information asymmetries peak. In other words, intense periods of IPO activity tend to occur when the takeover activity is relatively low and vice versa. This could help explain why IPO and going private may occur in negatively correlated waves.

market. In this case, we should include the delisting in the category of voluntary delisting.

The decision to leave the stock exchange does not necessarily imply that shares cease to be traded. A number of delisted firms end up being traded on Over-The-Counter (OTC) markets such as the OTC Bulletin Board, the Pink Sheets, and so on. These trading venues are not centralized markets but represent electronic inter-dealer quotation systems. The listing standards of these quotation systems are far more relaxed than those found in the official exchanges and sometimes they are not regulated at all.

Consequently, we can distinguish delisted firms depending on whether or not the shares continue to be traded. Firms *going private* are firms whose shares are no longer publicly traded while firms *going dark* are those companies whose shares are subsequently admitted to OTC markets. In addition, a firm could also choose to delist from one market and move to another venue due to reasons such as lower listing fees, less stringent disclosure requirements, and so on. This choice is different from going dark since the shares continue to be listed on centralized regulated markets. The shares only switch the venue, for example, from Main Markets to Second Markets or from the stock exchange of a country to the stock exchange of another country.

Although going private, going dark, and the transfer of the exchange venue may only appear to be different ways to delist a firm from technical and legal perspectives, these delisting processes show profound economic and financial differences in terms of theoretical motivations, effects on delisted firms, effects on their shares, and procedural differences. Equally profound differences can be found by comparing voluntary and involuntary delisting. The two classification criteria (i.e., voluntary vs. involuntary delisting and going private vs. going dark) may interact with each other in the sense that voluntary delisting typically takes the form of going private, but it does not exclude the possibility that a firm goes dark or changes the trading venue voluntarily. Conversely, involuntary delisting normally includes going dark and the transfer from a market to another, but it also comprises going private.

This book tries to answer the following questions: How, when, and why do firms go private? How, when, and why do firms go dark? How, when, and why do firms change the listing location? What are the consequences of going dark, going private, and the transfer of trading location on firms and shares? Is the evidence from the field consistent with the theory? If not, how can the result be explained?

1.2 Concepts and Definitions

Going private transactions which are also called public-to-private (PTP) transactions or minority freeze-outs describe a deal in which a quoted firm is taken private. Lehn and Poulsen (1989) define a going private transaction "*as one that converted a free-standing, publicly traded corporation into a privately held corporation*". The European Private Equity and Venture Capital Association provides a straightforward definition of PTP transactions that puts together the main elements characterizing the deal: "*A transaction involving an offer for the entire share capital of a listed target company by a new company—Newco—and the subsequent re-registration of that listed target company as a private company. The shareholders of Newco usually comprise members of the target company's management and private equity providers. Additional financing for the offer is normally provided by other debt providers*".

All PTP transactions therefore share two common attributes: (1) the public corporate ownership is fully replaced, implying a change of the corporate control; (2) after the transaction, the firm's shares are no longer publicly traded. PTP transactions can also be divided into more specific categories according to two distinctive criteria: (1) the identity of the investor that takes the firm private; (2) the scheme used to finance the deal.

Academicians and practitioners are used to referring to transactions as PTP when the firm is taken private through a merger or an acquisition performed by the incumbent management team (so-called Management Buyout, MBO) or a management team from outside the company (so-called Management Buy-in, MBI). In both cases, management may share the resulting equity ownership with outside private investors who help finance the acquisition of publicly traded shares. The unrestrained rise of private equity institutions since 2000 has resulted in the growth of Institutional Buyouts (IBO). In an IBO, the largest equity interest that follows the deal is held by a private equity investor[2] that may share the ownership with the existent management team or may install its own management.

Regardless of the identity of the investor performing the deal, a PTP transaction may be carried out through a number of legal arrangements such as the use of special purpose vehicles (SPV) also called shell corporations, wholly owned by the management and/or the private equity investor, in which the public firm is merged. The use of a shell corporation is also

[2] Private equity investors are typically funds structured as limited partnerships with outside investors who act as passive limited partners and the private equity firm that acts as the controlling general partner (Metrick and Yasuda 2010).

aimed at aiding the financing of the operation. From this perspective, a PTP transaction primarily financed by debt is ordinarily called Leveraged Buyout (LBO). Debt is normally raised by the shell corporation that uses the publicly traded shares as collateral. The target firm is subsequently merged into the shell corporation so that debt is attached to the target firm that ends up with a debt-burdened capital structure.

We can now formalize the main techniques used to go private (DeAngelo et al. 1984). First, a firm may go private through a *merger*. A going-private merger implies that the listed firm is combined with a shell corporation created purposely for the implementation of the deal. The shell corporation is entirely owned by a management team, a private equity investor, a group of private equity investors, or a combination of them. Under the merger agreement, the controlling shareholder of the shell corporation becomes the sole equity owner of the surviving firm. The public shareholders have to give up their shares and normally receive cash in return. They also have to vote in order to approve the merger. The percentage of outstanding voting stocks required to approve the deal depends on the State Company Law and the content of the corporate charter and the statute of the firm being taken private.

Second, a PTP transaction may be structured in the form of *asset sales*. In this case, the shell corporation buys all of the firm's assets for cash. The firm is subsequently liquidated by distributing cash to public shareholders. Alternatively, the firm may continue to exist as a closed-end fund that makes an immediate buyback tender offer after the asset sale. A PTP transaction in the form of asset sales also requires shareholder approval.

Third, a firm may be taken private through a *tender offer*. Unlike mergers and asset sales, going-private tender offers do not require a vote or the involuntary disposal of the stocks held by public shareholders unless a sufficient number of public shares are tendered.[3] The tender offer is generally made by the firm itself, an insider, or a corporation wholly owned by the management, or other private investors.

Finally, a company can go private as the result of a *reverse stock split*. This technique consists of reducing the number of outstanding shares in order

[3] In the US, the squeeze-out thresholds are regulated by State laws. For example, in Delaware, if the acquirer purchases at least 90% of the target's shares in the tender offer, it may then squeeze out the remaining shares with a short form merger, a merger that requires no further involvement by the target's board or stockholders. In other countries there are similar squeeze-out regulations. For example, in Germany and Italy, the squeeze-out threshold is 95% and in the UK it is 90%.

to lead the number of stockholders of record[4] below some thresholds required by the law to have shares publicly traded on the stock market. The fractional shares resulting from the reverse stock split are generally redeemed for cash. For example, if the company issues one new share for each 10,000 previously outstanding and a shareholder holds 5000 shares, the fractional interest, that is 0.50 of a share, is liquidated for cash. Sometimes the company gives shareholders the choice between cashing out and purchasing sufficient additional fractional interests to get a full post-reverse split share. Depending on the State law, a company's board of directors can deliberate a reverse stock split without seeking shareholder approval.

1.3 Going Private in the US: Regulations and Legislation

A firm that wants to go public has to prepare two main documents. First, Section 12(g)(1) of the Securities Exchange Act of 1934 states that every issuer which is engaged in interstate commerce, or in a business affecting interstate commerce, or whose securities are traded by use of the mails or any means or instrumentality of interstate commerce shall register such securities by filing with the Securities and Exchange Commission (SEC) a registration statement[5] with respect to such securities provided that:

[4] In the US, we need to distinguish *shareholders of record* from *beneficial shareholders*. The difference between the two concepts is a consequence of the fast dematerialization of shares pursued by the major stock exchanges in order to increase the efficiency of stock trading, brokerage, and clearing services (Marosi and Massoud 2007). The effect of this dematerialization process is that shareholders no longer hold paper share certificates. They hold their claims in electronic form with street names such as Goldman Sachs, Morgan Stanley, and other brokerage firms. Consequently, the number of shareholders listed in corporate records as having been issued a paper stock certificate has significantly reduced. This has also created a significant deviation between the number of *beneficial shareholders*, who are the actual shareholders, and the number of *shareholders of record*, who are the brokerage firms in which the beneficial shareholders hold their shares electronically. This means that Goldman Sachs, as the holder of the claims of thousands of beneficial shareholders, will be counted as one certificate holder (one shareholder of record). The Securities and Exchange Commission (SEC) only considers the number of shareholders of record in order to define the threshold below which a firm can delist and terminate the registration of securities under Section 12(g) of the Securities Exchange Act of 1934 that leads to the end of reporting obligations for listed firms. A formal definition of securities "held of record" is provided by the Rule 12g5-1 "Definition of securities 'held of record'" of the Code of Federal Regulations (Title 17, Chapter II, Part 240—General Rules and Regulations, Securities Exchange Act of 1934).

[5] Form 10 is the type of document that should be submitted to the SEC in order to make the registration statement.

1. the issuer has total assets exceeding $10 million, and
2. a class of equity security held of record by either 2000 persons or 500 persons who are not accredited investors.[6]

Second, in addition to the registration with the SEC, the issuer with shares publicly traded on a stock exchange has to register on a national security exchange by filing an application, by using the same form used for the registration with the SEC, with the exchange under Section 12(b) of the Securities Exchange Act of 1934. The registration form has to contain all the information on the firm such as business description, risk factors, financial information, directors, and executive officers, and so on.

Both registrations trigger a number of periodic reporting obligations under Section 12(b) and (g) such as annual report (Form 10-K), quarterly reports (Form 10-Q), current report (Form 8-K) for the communication of events relevant to a firm's shareholders, and so on.

The procedure for going private involves several steps. According to the Rule 12 g-4 "Certifications of termination of registration under Section 12(g)" of the Code of Federal Regulations (Title 17, Chapter II, Part 240), termination of registration of a class of securities under Section 12(g) of the Securities Exchange Act of 1934 shall take effect 90 days after the issuer certifies to the Securities and Exchange Commission (SEC) on Form 15[7] that the class of securities is held of record by:

1. less than 300 persons, or
2. less than 500 persons, where the total assets of the issuer have not exceeded $10 million on the last day of each of the issuer's most recent three fiscal years.

Deregistration by Form 15 should be accompanied by the submission of Form 25 whereby the firm notifies to the SEC the withdrawal of a class of securities from listing on a national securities exchange and from registration under Section 12(b). Both deregistrations lead to the termination of the periodic reporting obligations under Section 12(b) and (g).

[6] Accredited investors are mainly institutional investors, high-net-worth individuals, and directors-executive officers of the issuer. For a formal definition, see Rule 501 of the Code of Federal Regulations (Title 17, Chapter II, Part 230, General Rules and Regulations, Securities Act of 1933).

[7] Form 15 is the type of document that the firm eligible to be delisted should submit to the SEC in order to certify and notify the termination of registration of a class of securities under Section 12(g) of the Securities Exchange Act of 1934.

Unfortunately, the procedure is not as straightforward as it may appear because the SEC asks the firm that wants to go private for additional documents. Pursuant to the Rule 13e-3 "Going private transactions by certain issuers or their affiliates" of the Code of Federal Regulations (Title 17, Chapter II, Part 240), the issuer has to file with the SEC the Schedule 13E-3 or the Schedule TO in which the company has to provide a lot of information on the transaction (i.e., tender offer, reverse stock split, asset sales, merger) the effect of which is to make any class of equity securities of the issuer which is subject to Section 12(g) of the Securities Exchange Act of 1934 eligible for termination of registration under Rule 12g-4. Such document includes all the information a shareholder needs to understand the characteristics, purposes, motivations, effects, and fairness of the transaction. Moreover, if the transaction involves a tender offer or if the consideration is going to consist, in whole or in part, of securities of another issuer, disclosure under Regulations 14D, 14A, or 14C of the Code of Federal Regulations (Title 17, Chapter II, Part 240) will also be required.

The high transparency required in the deal is strictly related to the risks of insider self-dealing implied in the transaction itself. Typical issues triggered by the operation can be linked to the individual that initiates the transaction (are the majority shareholders driving the deal or is there an interested third party?), the financing method (will there be financing involved that will affect the firm's leverage and cash flow after the transaction?), the risk of litigation, and so on. Consequently, SEC tends to scrutinize PTP transactions closely.

1.4 Why Do Firms Go Private? Theoretical Models

The most straightforward approach to identifying the motivations underlying the decision to delist relies on two basic points (Bharath and Dittmar 2010). First, when a firm goes public, it should carry out a benefit-cost analysis. If this analysis shows that the advantages of having shares publicly traded on a stock market exceed the costs then the firm should decide to list its shares, otherwise, it should continue to be privately held. The benefit-cost analysis can be conducted at any time after the listing and if it results in a reversal of the trade-off between costs and benefits (i.e., costs higher than benefits), then the firm should opt out of the stock market.

Second, the approach based on reversing costs and benefits of the listing can work because most of them are actually reversible. If so, we can draw on the theories that provide the motivations of going public to get insight into going private. Put differently, by systematically reversing many of the predictions of the going-public theories, we can determine the factors that can influence the choice between being a private or a public firm. Of course, this does not exclude the possibility of modeling further ad hoc motivations of why a firm may decide to go private. Consequently, the theoretical reasons for going private will be classified into groups according to both the forces triggering the decision and the fact that these forces either come from reversing a going-public determinant or are not directly related to the going-public decision.

1.4.1 Information-Based Theories

These theories link the decision to go private to information asymmetries between managers and investors that characterize publicly traded firms and affect the costs and benefits of being a public firm. Generally speaking, when a firm has shares that are diffusely held and publicly traded on the stock market, firm managers are likely to hold more information about the current state and the future prospects of the company than the suppliers of capital, especially the equity providers. The acquisition of information by investors is required in order to value the company. However, gathering information could be a costly process and an investor, especially a retail investor, may find the effort needed to get the information to be too much. Without information, the investor could be induced not to trade on the stock market. This results in at least two consequences. First, information gaps lead to valuation gaps. Second, the security market price no longer aggregates information effectively due to a lack of liquidity. How can the insufficient information transfer affect the decision to go private? Some information-based considerations will be provided.

Adverse Selection

According to Akerlof (1970) and Leland and Pyle (1977), the lack of circulation of information between sellers and buyers may prevent the market from performing properly. Let's suppose firms have to finance several projects whose quality is variable. Although managers and entrepreneurs know the true quality of projects, investors, without the needed information, cannot distinguish between high-quality projects and low-quality projects. Market value therefore reflects the average project quality.

Now suppose that the market places an average value on projects that is higher than the average cost. This causes firms with low-quality projects to make profits by supplying a large amount of shares in order to foist them on uninformed investors. The intention to sell shares leads uninformed investors to revise downward their valuation on the average quality of projects. Consequently, buyers will be unwilling to buy shares unless the selling price is heavily discounted as well. The last consequence is that firms which are known (by the managers) to make good projects and deserve to be financed cannot sell shares because they know that any attempt to sell shares would convey to the market the information that they are trying to sell a "lemon". Consequently, the quality of firms selling shares and the quality of their projects will be both low. This result is known as an *adverse selection problem* because the quality of firms that try to sell shares is worse than average. For firms with good projects to be financed, information transmission must occur.

This concept can be transferred easily to the IPO market. When a firm decides to go public this triggers investors' concerns that they might be buying a "lemon". Their concerns, in turn, adversely affect both the average quality of firms seeking a new listing and the price at which their shares can be sold initially and during the public life of the firm. Leland and Pyle (1977) demonstrate that the entrepreneur that invests a great deal of his own wealth in his own projects can signal their higher quality.

They show, in their Theorems I and II, that entrepreneurs are motivated to hold a higher fraction of ownership in more profitable projects and that the market reads higher entrepreneurial ownership as a signal of more favorable projects. Moreover, the entrepreneur will make larger investments in their own projects than would be the case if they could costlessly communicate their true mean value. This means that if the communication to the market of the true mean value of the project can be effected at a low cost, the fraction of equity in the project held by the entrepreneur will be low as well. However, less costly communication may not be available and the only way to send a credible signal to the market can consist in showing that it is in the self-interest of the entrepreneur to send true signals. The holding of a significant equity share in the project is a way to communicate to the market of being self-interested in sending a flawless signal of the true average value of the project.

Privately held firms should not suffer significant adverse selection problems. First, shares of privately held firms are rarely issued to or traded by outside investors. They are typically bought by the entrepreneur and/or members of his family that know the quality of the firm's projects. Second, an entrepreneur in a privately held firm normally holds a large fraction of its equity. This would convey positive information regarding the firm's projects and should reduce adverse selection costs. Given the lower adverse selection problems affecting private firms, which types of firms should go private?

The answer depends on the factors influencing the intensity of adverse selection costs. Firms in which these factors play an important role are more likely to go private. Adverse selection costs are not uniform across firms but depend on some firm characteristics that can exacerbate or lessen these costs.

A first characteristic is the firm size. Small firms are more difficult to value for investors than large firms due to lower information transparency and visibility.[8] A second characteristic is the firm's age. Young firms are more difficult to value for investors than old firms as a result of insufficient track record of financial information and uncertainty regarding future growth opportunities. A third characteristic is the industry. High-tech firms are more difficult to value for investors than firms operating in more traditional sectors due to higher uncertainty regarding future cash flows. Any other factor that makes it more difficult to estimate firm value can increase adverse selection costs. Small, young firms operating in technology-based industries are more likely to go private in order to avoid the severe adverse selection costs they would face if their shares continued to be listed.

Information Production Cost

Chemmanur and Fulghieri (1999) develop a model of the going-public decision that takes into account explicitly the trade-off underlying a firm's choice between remaining private or going public. Let's assume that an entrepreneur has to finance a positive net present value (NPV) project by external capital providers. They focus on three key differences between private and public firms when financing this project. First, in the case of public firms, the resources required to finance the project come from selling shares to a large number of investors, whereas in the case of private firms, much of the external financing is provided by one large investor (e.g., a venture capitalist) or a small group of investors.

[8] Small firms tend to be more opaque in providing information on their business as a result of costs related to disclosure requirements, investor relations, and potential loss of competitive advantage (Pettit and Singer 1985). Moreover, they also tend to be followed by few analysts and their shares are often neglected by large institutional investors (Freeman 1987; Draper and Paudyal 2008).

This has several consequences: first, the presence of a large number of equity suppliers in public firms implies that these shareholders are much better diversified than those in private firms. Second, the higher ownership concentration in private firms entails that a large investor or a small group of large investors will hold significantly higher bargaining power against the entrepreneur in such a firm than small, dispersed investors in a public firm. Second, in a public firm, the entrepreneur has to convince a much larger group of investors that the project deserves to be financed. This means that any cost borne by these outside investors in evaluating the quality of the firm's project will be shifted to the firm in the form of a higher cost of capital and a lower share price. Third, for public firms, the magnitude of the total costs incurred by outside equity holders in evaluating the quality of the project will be reduced by many unsophisticated investors being able to free ride on the information they can infer from the publicly observable price at which shares are sold to the market.

The above framework results in a clear trade-off between public and private firms. On the one hand, selling shares to a single large shareholder has the advantage of minimizing the information production cost since such an investor evaluates the project only once and contributes entirely to the capital required to finance it. The disadvantage is that this large investor does not reach full diversification and wields considerably more bargaining power against the entrepreneur than public shareholders. Consequently, a higher cost of capital is likely to be charged by such a large investor. On the other hand, raising the resources required to finance the project by issuing shares to a large number of investors has the advantage that each investor is fully diversified and has almost no bargaining power relative to the entrepreneur since the shares are priced in a competitive equity market. The disadvantage is that the presence of many investors could result in some form of duplication in information production and, consequently, the entrepreneur is likely to bear a larger aggregate information production cost.

How can this trade-off be settled? The factor that can tip the scale in favor of being public or private is represented by the magnitude of outsiders' information production costs. On the one hand, we have large, established firms that are well known by outsiders. For these firms, information production costs are low because outsiders can acquire information on them without bearing significant costs as a result of information accumulated over time in the public domain. These firms, in equilibrium, should go public since the higher diversification by investors and the absence of bargaining power against the entrepreneur weigh more than the problems related to the duplication in information production.

On the other hand, we have young firms. They are less known and investors have to struggle more in order to acquire information on them. This implies higher information production costs and the problem of duplication in information production outweighs the benefits of being a public firm (i.e., higher diversification by investors and no bargaining power against the entrepreneur). These firms, in equilibrium, should raise funds from a few large private investors such as venture capitalists in order to minimize the outsiders' combined evaluation cost.

Chemmanur and Fulghieri (1999) also show that the age and size of a firm are not the only variables that can explain the going-public decision in an information-based environment. Capital intensity and technological uncertainty of a firm can also be related to the listing choice. The intuition behind them is as follows. When a firm's capital requirement increases, we have two effects: first, the expected return required by the large private investor (e.g., the venture capitalist) increases as well, therefore lowering the price at which each share will be sold to the venture capitalist. The logic is that the higher the capital intensity of a firm, the higher the fraction of equity that the firm has to offer to the venture capitalist in return for the financing required. Consequently, the venture capitalist, being risk averse and less than fully diversified, will demand a greater cost of capital for committing a larger portion of his wealth in a given firm.

Second, at the same time, the price per share of equity sold by the firm with good projects in the public equity market increases since when the capital intensity increases, the cost imposed on the firm with bad projects that tries to mimic the firm with good projects increases as well. The logic can be explained as follows.[9] Let's suppose we have two types of firms: firms with good projects and firms with bad projects. Since the firms with bad projects try to offer shares at the same price at which the shares are sold by the firms with good projects, they will be able to raise only a fraction of the whole amount of resources they desire, given that only some information producers buy shares in this case. The consequence is that they will be forced to scale down their projects and forego their NPV.

Accordingly, this sequence of events occurs in the firm with bad projects: (1) the higher the capital intensity, (2) the larger the desired external financing amount, (3) the greater the magnitude of the shortfall in the amount actually raised, (4) the higher the need to scale down the projects, (5) the greater the amount of NPV foregone. Consequently, the equilibrium pooling

[9] For an analytical formalization of the model, see Chemmanur and Fulghieri (1999).

price for the firm with good projects will be higher since the frequency with which firms with bad projects pool with firms with good projects decreases as a result of the higher mimicking costs.

Technological uncertainty comes into play as follows. The risk premium required by the venture capitalist for investing in industries characterized by greater technological uncertainty is larger. These firms should therefore go public with a higher probability at an earlier stage in their life.

How can we convert the above framework into a going-private decision model? Let's suppose a firm has shares that are already publicly traded on the stock market. According to Chemmanur and Fulghieri (1999), this firm should remain listed as long as the benefits coming from portfolio diversification and the absence of bargaining power outweigh the costs of duplication in information production. Which factor(s) can reverse this trade-off? At the beginning of the discussion on information-based models, we stated that market price has the power to aggregate information on the firm. Besides, the fact that it is publicly observable by outside investors reduces the total evaluation costs that such investors have to bear in order to assess the firm and its projects.

With a publicly observable market price, only a fraction of investors will incur the information production cost since the market price conveys information across investors. Some amount of duplication in information acquisition cannot be avoided, but the observable market price allows investors to significantly reduce the degree of such duplication.

Based on this setting, two main factors can reverse the trade-off in favor of the going-private choice: first, the growth in information production costs; second, the inability of the market price to reflect and convey information successfully. Consequently, the prediction of this model is that the lower the market liquidity, the higher the probability of going private will be since the market price may no longer aggregate and convey information effectively. This means that firms with illiquid shares are more likely to go private. Likewise, firms with a large amount of R&D expenditures or ones that significantly increase these expenditures over time are more likely to go private as a result of higher evaluation costs.

The same logic applies to firms which, for example, experience a decrease in the analyst coverage, significantly reduce their size, have a low institutional ownership, and are listed in countries with a limited presence of intermediaries engaged in working with and producing information on companies, and so on. Moreover, project evaluation difficulty being equal (i.e., information production costs are the same), firms in less capital intensive industries are more likely to go private. Likewise, capital intensity being equal, firms in industries in which projects are intrinsically more difficult to evaluate (i.e., this means that information production costs are higher) are more likely to go private. It is worth noting that the model based on information production cost leads to predictions comparable to those proposed by the adverse selection perspective.

An information production cost model is extensible in order to identify other situations that can promote/hinder the going-private decision. For example, the hot issue market phenomenon (Ritter 1984) is explained by Chemmanur and Fulghieri (1999) in terms of productivity shock in an industry. They argue that a productivity shock will increase the value of a firm with good projects so that if a firm in the industry that experiences a productivity shock chooses to go public, the benefit to a participant in its IPO of producing information is larger. This increases the proportion of informed investors and, in turn, *increases* the threshold of information production costs after which the firm prefers to remain private.

The implication is that a productivity shock in an industry increases the probability that many firms go public simultaneously. We argue that the contrary may also be true. A productivity shock in an industry may also *reduce* the threshold of evaluation costs of firms already listed. As a result, we could see many firms in an industry that go private simultaneously.

Another extension is related to the effect of listing requirements to the decision to go public. According to their model, the imposition by a stock exchange of more stringent listing requirements can be interpreted as a requisite regarding the minimum amount of information on the firm that has to be available to the public before the firm can be listed, therefore imposing an upper bound on the outsiders' cost of information production. This could affect the decision between going public or remaining private. In this case too, the opposite may also be true for firms that are already quoted. A change of listing requirements could affect the decision between going private or remaining public as a result of the modification of the upper bound on the outsiders' information production costs.[10]

[10] The issue of the effect of a modification of the listing requirements on the going private decision is directly analyzed by Engel et al. (2007) who investigate how the enactment of the Sarbanes-Oxley Act of 2002 affected the decision to go private. They find that higher disclosure requirements imposed by the new regulation induced many small and poorly liquid firms to leave the stock market because the benefits of greater transparency, lower information acquisition costs, and higher liquidity were surpassed by the costs of compliance that each firm had to bear. The model proposed by Chemmanur and Fulghieri (1999) takes into

Serendipitous Information Production

In their model, Chemmanur and Fulghieri (1999) do not distinguish between the type of information investors can collect in the sense that they assume information production to be costly indiscriminately. Subrahmanyam and Titman (1999) modify the information structure assuming that there is a new information component on the future payoff both on the assets in place and from future growth opportunities of a firm. The new information component is characterized by the fact that it can be obtained by investors serendipitously, that is, by luck and without cost. Market investors therefore come across serendipitous information by chance. For example, investors can acquire information on the aggregate demand for a firm's product if they come across information regarding how well the products are liked by its customers.

This new information structure allows for the presence on the stock market of two types of informed investors: on the one hand, those that trade on the market based on information collected expensively; on the other hand, those that trade on the market based on information collected serendipitously. What is the effect of the latter traders on the trade-off between going public or remaining private? Which insights can we gain into the going private decision? The model proposed by Subrahmanyam and Titman (1999) does not differ from that proposed by Chemmanur and Fulghieri (1999) in a lot of predictions, but it takes into account a new information structure that affects the decision to go public. In what follows, we briefly summarize the model and its results and focus on how it provides us with insights both for the going-public and the going-private choice.

Let's assume the presence of N traders that receive a serendipitous information signal described by a random variable of the form $\theta + \eta_j$, $j = 1,\ldots,N$, where η_j is i.i.d. across the serendipitously informed traders, and M traders expending time and effort in collecting a costly signal described by a random variable of the form $\delta + \xi + \epsilon_i$, $i = 1,\ldots,M$, where ϵ_i is i.i.d. across the traders who acquire costly information. The random variables expressing costly and serendipitous signals have the following characteristics:

consideration this aspect with a focus on the upper bound on the investors' information production costs resulting from the introduction of such a regulation. We will come back both to the relationship between going private and listing requirements and to the trade-off between the costs of disclosure requirements and their benefits to investors in terms of lower information acquisition costs, lower adverse selection problems, and higher liquidity, later on in the text.

- let υ_δ and υ_θ be the variances, respectively, of the costly and serendipitous signal;
- let υ_ϵ and υ_η be the common variances of the uncorrelated error terms, respectively, in the costly and serendipitous signal; and
- let υ_ξ be the variance of the correlated error term in the costly signal.

Based on this framework related to the main characteristics of the market and information structure, Subrahmanyam and Titman (1999) obtain the following key results.[11]

The Process by Which Information Is Incorporated into the Value of Publicly Traded Shares

If $\upsilon_\epsilon = 0$ (we are therefore supposing that costly signals are perfectly correlated across investors), the higher the number of traders collecting costly signals (*M*), the higher the market liquidity will be. This result is intuitive: if traders with a particular type of information observe perfectly correlated signals, increasing their number leads to an intensification of competition, therefore increasing market liquidity and efficiency. On the contrary, if υ_ϵ is strictly positive (we are therefore assuming that costly information is diverse across informed investors), increasing their number can lead to two opposing effects: on the one hand, competition between these traders increases (market liquidity grows); on the other hand, the pool of information increases as well (market liquidity decreases).

Subrahmanyam and Titman (1999) demonstrate that competition effect dominates information effect, therefore increasing market liquidity and efficiency, when *M* is sufficiently high. The same intuition applies to informed investors that obtain a serendipitous signal: for sufficiently large *N*, an increase in the number of investors with serendipitous information improves market liquidity and efficiency.

The Interaction Between Serendipitous Information and Costly Information

Given that the number of investors with costly information (*M*) is endogenous because it depends on several exogenous factors such as υ_δ, υ_θ, and *N*, this requires an analysis of the effect of serendipitous information on

[11] For a rigorous analytical demonstration of these results, see Subrahmanyam and Titman (1999).

costly information acquisition. Therefore the question we have to ask is, how can the number of serendipitously informed traders (N) affect the profits of traders with costly information? Subrahmanyam and Titman (1999) demonstrate that an increase in N will increase market liquidity and the number of traders with costly information (and their profits) if the initial number of serendipitously informed traders (N) is large enough. Otherwise, if the initial value of N is small, an increase in N can crowd out costly informed traders.

The Interaction Between Information Content of a Firm's Stock Price, the Amount of Capital Invested in Growth Opportunities, and Their Value

Subrahmanyam and Titman (1999) demonstrate that the expected value of the payoff from growth opportunities is increasing in v_δ and v_θ, for given values of N and M. This implies that for a given level of informed trading, the expected value of growth opportunities is higher when information is more valuable. Besides, lowering the cost of information increases the expected value of growth opportunities. These relationships lead to the following main results: (1) if costly signals are perfectly correlated ($v_\epsilon = 0$), then although an increase in N decreases M, the net effect of these changes on the expected value of growth opportunities is always positive; (2) if v_ϵ is strictly positive, an increase in N results in an increase in the expected value of growth opportunities only if N is large enough. In contrast, if N is small, increasing N results in a decrease in M and the effect on the expected value of growth opportunities is ambiguous.

The link between investment decisions and the information content of the stock price therefore depends on whether the costly information is diverse or strongly correlated across traders. If costly information is perfectly correlated, the poorer investment decisions that come from crowding out investors with costly information are dominated by the benefits of increased serendipitous information. On the contrary, if costly information is diverse across traders, it reduces the intensity of competition among traders with costly information (M decreases) with deleterious effects on the expected value of growth opportunities.

The Choice Between Public and Private Financing: Some Insights from the Model

Based on the previous results, we can draw some insights into the choice between public and private financing.

1. *If costly signals are perfectly correlated* ($v_\epsilon = 0$), without serendipitously informed traders the firm always chooses to remain private. The reason behind this result is that without traders with serendipitous information, the cost of duplication in information production (Chemmanur and Fulghieri 1999) dominates, without the benefit of serendipitously informed traders. This duplication is absent in private financing.
2. *If* v_ϵ *is strictly positive*, the firm chooses public financing even when $N = 0$ provided that M is large enough. The reason is that if costly information is diverse across traders, the stock market aggregates a large number of costly diverse signals. In this case, the benefits of public financing outweigh those of private financing.
3. *However, if* v_ϵ *is strictly positive*, the relationship between the benefits of public financing and the number of serendipitously informed traders *is not monotonically positive* in the sense that an increase in N *does not always increase* the benefits of going public. The reason is that if N is initially small and serendipitous information is sufficiently diverse across traders ($v_\eta > 0$), as already shown, an increase in N decreases market liquidity and the number of traders with costly information (M) and can make private financing preferred over the public one.

The Trade-Off Between Going Public or Remaining Private: A Summary of Scenarios

All in all, a firm that is publicly financed will have a higher value than a firm that is privately financed; therefore there will be a greater propensity to go public, when:

1. the cost of information tends to be small (or M tends to be large): cheap information makes the problem of duplication in information production less severe. This increases the appeal of going public;
2. N increases: the higher the number of serendipitously informed traders, the higher the market liquidity and efficiency, the higher the benefits of public financing will be. In this case the crowding out effect does not exist and the relationship between the benefits of going public and the number of serendipitously informed traders is monotonically positive because we assume M to be large (or the cost of information to be small);
3. v_θ increases: the higher the variance of serendipitous information, the higher the value of information will be. This implies that public financing will be more attractive;

4. υ_ϵ increases: the larger the diversity of costly information across traders, the higher the benefits of having diverse information aggregated by the stock market will be. This makes public financing more appealing.

The above effects make the relationship between the benefits of public financing and the number of serendipitously informed traders *monotonically positive*. This means that the crowding out effect does not work.

However, while υ_θ and cost of information are *always* monotonically related to the benefits of going public, N and υ_ϵ can have ambiguous relationships with the benefits of public financing. First, as already shown, increasing N can crowd out costly informed investors, therefore reducing their number and market liquidity with detrimental effects on the benefits of going public, when N is initially small and υ_η is great. A large υ_η means that serendipitous information is more diverse across investors therefore leading to lower benefits of such information on firm value. In this case the deleterious effect of the crowding out (a decrease in M) dominates. On the other hand, when N is significantly large, the benefits of greater serendipitous information dominate the crowding out effect. Second, a similar non-monotonic relationship can be found with reference to υ_ϵ.

The increase in υ_ϵ will have three effects: (1) a large υ_ϵ implies that the benefits of having diverse costly information aggregated by the stock market are large as well (greater attractiveness of public financing); (2) a large υ_ϵ can also result in a decrease in M because fewer investors find it valuable to collect more diverse information. Put differently, when υ_ϵ increases, the intensity of competition between informed investors decreases as a result of the larger diversity of their information (lower attractiveness of public financing); (3) for a given M, υ_ϵ also affects market liquidity. The effect is negative for low υ_ϵ and positive for high υ_ϵ (ambiguous effect on the attractiveness of public financing). These three effects influence the convenience of going public over remaining private in a non-monotonic way: a firm will go public only for intermediate levels of υ_ϵ.

Empirical Implications and Intuitions for the Going Private Decision

1. Public financing becomes more attractive when the market for a firm's product expands and future demand uncertainty increases. We should therefore find a higher likelihood of going public when a firm's sales increase (this result is empirically found by Pagano et al. 1998). In this case, the probability that an investor can come across

serendipitous information increases (in the model, v_θ is larger). This means that in industries characterized by higher demand uncertainty and expanding markets, serendipitous information should play an important role. As a result, for example, Internet and biotech firms are more likely to go public. However, for these firms, costly information is less available and, according to the model, the benefits of going public are reduced. A consequence is that, in order to make going public attractive, N and v_θ should be large enough to dominate the costly information effect.

This intuition can be reversed: listed firms in industries with contracting markets and highly predictable future demand are more likely to go private as a result of the minor role of serendipitous information. However, in industries with these characteristics, costly information is likely to be highly available, thereby increasing the attractiveness of public financing. The convenience of going private requires N and v_θ to be relatively small in order to significantly reduce the serendipitous information effect.

2. In firms that require asset or capital structure restructuring, serendipitous information is not likely to play an important role. Information on this type of firm is better obtained by a large private capital provider through costly and valuable analysis of the firm. Consequently, listed firms that intend to undergo a reorganization are more likely to go private. This could help explain why a large number of buyouts anticipate internal reorganization plans effected after the firm has gone private.
3. The model proposed by Subrahmanyam and Titman (1999) also shows that if the cost of becoming an active trader and the cost of information acquisition are small, public financing becomes more attractive, therefore increasing the number of firms that find it convenient to list their shares. This, in turn, increases the size of the stock market, its liquidity and its efficiency which induce more and more firms to go public and create a domino effect. Without incentives and stimuli that trigger the snowballing effect, the stock market cannot reach the critical mass that allows this effect to spread.

This snowballing effect could help explain some empirical observations. For example, Comment and Jarrell (1995) show that since the 1980s, firms in the US have been selling and spinning off divisions, reducing the importance of internal capital markets, and increasing the importance of public capital markets. Over the same time period, IPOs have reached exceptional levels. In this case, the triggering effect that has increased market size and liquidity was the tendency of large conglomerates to spin off divisions in order to become more focused. A similar effect occurred in the US stock market in response to the decrease in brokerage commissions in 1975 (Bhide 1990). More recently, the fast growth of some stock markets in emerging economies may be related to stimulating actions taken by local governments on stock exchanges. For example, the governments of many emerging countries put into effect a number of privatizations of state-owned firms that have increased market capitalization (Perotti and Van Oijen 2001).

Likewise, in the same spirit as moves that make going public more attractive, the significant number of delisted firms since 2000 could be related to events that have stimulated going private, creating a snowballing effect. For example, the Sarbanes-Oxley Act of 2002 has made the disclosure requirements of listed firms far more stringent. A lot of firms, especially the small and less liquid ones, responded to this new regulation by delisting their shares from the stock market as a result of increased costs (Engel et al. 2007). Bankruptcy and the ensuing delisting of a large number of Internet firms could also have induced such a snowballing effect.

Information Acquisition Costs and the Value of Confidentiality

Subrahmanyam and Titman (1999) as well as Chemmanur and Fulghieri (1999) developed a model in which the lower the information acquisition costs to investors, the higher the price at which firms can sell their shares to the public market, the higher the market liquidity, and the higher the benefits of public financing. However, when a firm disseminates information on its business and strategies that investors can collect by chance or expensively, it is likely to bear a loss of competitive advantage in the sense that the disclosure of information can decrease the value of a project and, at the same time, may trigger undesirable actions by the firm's competitors who may profit from this information (Campbell 1979; Yosha, 1995). Yosha (1995) proposes a model that demonstrates that when a firm has sensitive information, that is, information whose public dissemination can be deleterious to the firm value, it should prefer to remain private. In contrast, firms with less sensitive information are more likely to go public.

Yosha (1995)'s analysis distinguishes between bilateral and multilateral financing arrangements. The former can be thought of as private financing (e.g., venture capitalist) and the latter can be thought of as public financing. On the one hand, multilateral arrangements require the firm to provide a detailed documentation in order to allow the different capital providers to assess the quality of its projects needed to induce investors to buy its shares. On the other hand, bilateral arrangements are characterized by a higher level of confidentiality in the sense that information on the firm is provided to a single capital supplier. This implies that, in the first case, information is likely to become available to undesirable third parties such as the firm's competitors whereas in the second case, the probability of leakage of information is very small.

Yosha (1995) assumes the presence of two types of firms: innovator (firm with sensitive information that has to collect resources to finance a new and innovative project) and competitor (firm that can observe the actions of innovator and react consequently). According to Yosha (1995), the innovator's choice between private and public financing is based on the following considerations.[12] Private financing is less costly because it entails a lower dissemination of information. However, being confidential, it may trigger a strong response from competitors who believe that the innovator is tapping into private financing in order to hide sensitive information and, therefore, the fact that the quality of its project is higher than it actually is.

In contrast, public financing is costlier because it disseminates more information on the innovator's project. However, it entails a credible disclosure of private information. Consequently, if the quality of the innovator's project is not actually better, it would be worthwhile bearing the higher costs of public financing in order not to be perceived as being of a higher quality than it actually is.[13] On the other hand, if the quality of the innovator's project is better, it prefers private financing so that it is perceived as being of a lower quality than it is and also avoiding the costs of public financing in terms of a stronger reaction from the competitor.[14]

[12] For an analytical formalization of the model, see Yosha (1995).

[13] The intuition is that, in this case, the private information is publicly disclosed but the reaction of the competitor is not strong because the quality of the innovator's project is not high. The innovator therefore prefers to bear the higher costs of public financing rather than being perceived as being of high quality, therefore triggering a strong reaction from the competitor.

[14] In this case, the innovator prefers private financing because a public disclosure of private information on the project may trigger a stronger reaction from the competitor.

Implications for the Going Private Decision

The previous discussion leads to a number of empirical implications related to the delisting choice.

1. If a firm's quality is positively related to the degree of private (sensitive) information regarding its projects (Yosha 1995 assumes that the higher the level of sensitive information, the higher the quality of a firm's projects will be), we should find that highly innovative firms are more inclined to delist their shares from the public market in order to conceal private information on their projects from the market competitors and avoid their stronger reaction. This means that listed firms that embark on new and innovative projects should consider the opportunity to protect private information on these projects by delisting their shares, therefore gaining access to private financing. Consequently, firms with high levels of R&D expenditures should be more likely to go private. Likewise, firms that significantly increase their R&D investments over time should consider going private as well.
2. Listed firms that undertake a reorganization of their business should also consider going private in order to avoid revealing sensitive information regarding the reorganization plan to competitors. For example, firms that intend to initiate M&A plans and important product or geographical expansion plans in order to significantly improve their position in the market, should evaluate the possibility of delisting their shares before starting the strategy.
3. In the above situations, announcements of PTP transactions should be followed by a positive stock market response. The positive market reaction should reflect the value of these high-quality initiatives.

Investor Recognition

Merton (1987), in his essay on capital market equilibrium with incomplete information, demonstrates that one of the variables affecting a firm's value is the so-called degree of investor recognition, that is, the size of the investor base. Investor recognition can be meant as the extent to which shares of a firm are known and held by diverse shareholders. Merton (1987)'s intuition is quite straightforward[15]: before making portfolio

[15] For an analytical demonstration of these results, see Merton (1987).

decisions, investors have to get and process costly information regarding the firm. Investors that are not aware of the firm in the sense that they do not possess and process such information will not become shareholders of the firm. Moreover, he also shows that, in equilibrium, the higher the investor base, the lower the expected return on a security will be.

This implies that, all other things being equal, expected returns will tend to be lower on better-known firms with relatively larger investor bases. Consequently, an increase in the size of the firm's investor base is in the best interests of the current shareholders who benefit from a growth in firm value. Assuming that the management of a firm makes its decisions in the interests of the existing shareholders and that this interest can be best served by maximizing the current market value of the firm, we infer that management should expend resources of the firm in order to expand investor recognition by inducing investors who are not currently shareholders to incur the necessary costs of becoming aware of the firm.

The effect of inflating investor base on expected return and firm value tends to be greater for lesser-known firms. This result is intuitive: a large, established firm is likely to have an investor base that is already sufficiently large. Consequently, a further expansion will decrease the cost of capital to a limited extent and the management will also have less room to increase it significantly. The relationship between a firm's investor base and its cost of capital will also affect the firm's investment decisions. If the investor base increases, the cost of capital will fall and it will be optimal for the firm to increase the amount of investments. An increase in investments, in turn, will also result in a growth of the firm's size. The contrary is also true: if other events cause the firm to increase investments, the firm will also be willing to expand its investor base. In sum, providing the additional capital for new investments will often require the firm to issue new shares in order to expand investor recognition.

The above considerations lead to some empirical implications. First, firms that are neglected by sophisticated investors and analysts tend to have a higher expected return and a lower market value (Arbel et al. 1983). This could help explain why many small firms, little known by the investment community, trade at a discount. These firms are likely to bear a sort of free rider problem in the sense that investors, including the more sophisticated ones, are reluctant to invest in less known firms in order not to face the higher costs related to lower liquidity, difficulty in information acquisition, research costs, and marketing costs associated with educating investors about the benefits of investing in neglected stocks.

A money manager who wants to specialize in investing in these neglected firms should have the possibility of charging fees that are high enough to recover these costs. Otherwise, it chooses not to invest in them. A direct consequence of this evidence is represented by the benefits of being in the spotlight through newspapers and other mass media that allow the firm to be reached by a large investor base. This provides a rationale for expenditures on advertising the firm that is targeted for investors and on public relations designed to generate stories about the firm in the financial press.

What can we learn about the choice to go private? Firms that are disregarded by the investment community are more likely to go private because the higher cost of capital they have to pay does not allow them to maximize shareholder wealth. The management of these firms should endeavor to improve their visibility in order to expand the investor base, especially the institutional one, reduce the cost of capital, and increase the firm value. If this is not possible (e.g., the firm is overlooked because it does not have enough news to induce investors who are not currently shareholders to follow and trade the firm's securities), the management should evaluate the opportunity to delist the firm's shares.

Second, another empirical implication of Merton (1987)'s model is related to the ownership structure of the firm. According to its model, firms with highly concentrated ownership structures should be more likely to go private. The reasoning is that these firms are likely to have an investor base that is smaller than that of firms with a more diffused ownership structure, unless the largest shareholder is, for example, a fund with thousands of shareholders that, in this way, indirectly hold stocks of listed firms. This implies a higher cost of capital and a lower market value for less-widely held firms that could find it more convenient to go private.

While for neglected firms the expansion of investor base is a matter of information, for firms with high ownership concentration, achieving the aim of enlarging the investor base appears to be far less complicated. It would be sufficient to increase the degree of ownership dispersion either by selling stocks held by the largest shareholder or by selling newly issued shares to new investors. The effect of both actions would be a reduction in ownership concentration that, in the presence of a controlling shareholder, would expose the largest shareholder to the risk of losing control. Consequently, the largest shareholder could be unwilling to increase the investor base in order to avoid the risk of loss of control even if it were in the best interests of other shareholders.

Moreover, the standard mechanism to perform seasoned equity offerings (SEO) contemplated by the law in many countries, especially European ones, is represented by rights offerings to existing shareholders in contrast to public offerings. Rights issues are made in order to counter problems such as adverse selection, underinvestment, wealth transfers, ownership dilution, and so on (Eckbo and Masulis 1992, 1995). In a rights issue, current shareholders are given short-term warrants to purchase shares on a pro rata basis (i.e., proportionate to their existing ownership position), at a specified exercise price, generally lower than the current market price, until a designated expiration date. To the extent that newly issued shares are subscribed by the firm's current stockholders, a rights offering does not affect the investor base and prevents the firm from increasing ownership dispersion, thereby hampering the resulting positive effects on the cost of capital and firm value.[16]

The firm should therefore consider alternative issuing mechanisms, such as offers in which the underwriter is a guarantor, that allow the firm to get benefits similar to those offered by a rights issue, but with more chances that new shares could be placed in the other-than-existing shareholders' portfolios. Finally, other tactics to increase investor base consist, for example, of splitting stocks in order to attract, small, typically unsophisticated investors or reducing the minimum trading unit.

To sum up, Merton (1987)'s model predicts that neglected firms and those characterized by high ownership concentration are more likely to go private, the former as a result of a lower investor base following their low visibility, the latter as a result of a lower investor base resulting from a high ownership concentration. Neglected firms should undertake efforts to increase their visibility by improving the quality of their investor relations. Firms with highly concentrated ownership structures should try to expand ownership diffusion. Splitting stocks and reducing the minimum trading lot size are other techniques. If these attempts are not feasible, the decision to go private becomes an option that management should take into account in the best interests of the firm's current shareholders.

[16] Despite the fact that rights offerings have lower direct costs (i.e., fees) than public ones (Slovin et al. 2000), parallel research streams found that this method can be more expensive than a public offering due to indirect costs: (1) costs borne by shareholders to trade the rights (Hansen 1988); (2) lower market liquidity resulting from a rights offer due to the preserved higher ownership concentration (Kothare 1997); (3) wealth transfers from shareholders to convertible securities holders connected with non-neutral anti-dilution clauses (Myhal 1990); (4) possible agency costs induced by collusion between managers and underwriters (Smith 1977; Herman 1981); (5) stock price declining during the offering period, due to arbitrage activity frequently carried out by the underwriter (Singh 1997).

1.4.2 Investment Policy

Going public is generally considered a watershed moment in a firm's history since it is associated with a number of important changes in the firm. Once a firm is traded publicly, there is a wide market in which executives and other insiders can sell their shares. Consequently, it is reasonable to believe that, first, at least a portion of the funds raised during the offering are employed to finance new investments, second, capital-starved firms, with greater investment opportunities, are more likely to go public to tap into wide equity and debt public capital markets.

We should therefore find growth in a firm's investments in the years following the offering. This issue, which is theoretically clear, does not appear to be equally evident in empirical investigations. Pagano et al. (1998), in a sample of Italian IPOs, find that investments do not increase following the IPO, suggesting that demand for capital is not a major reason for going public. Contrasting evidence is found by Kim and Weisbach (2008) in an international sample of IPOs. They find that capital raised in IPOs is used to fund new investments, both in R&D and in tangible assets.

The intuition for the going-private choice is that when a firm lacks investment opportunities and its demand for new resources is poor, access to public markets becomes a less valuable option, whose disadvantages could overcome its advantages. In this case, the firm may opt to go private.

The same result, but with an explanation that is not related to the greater capital amount demanded by firms with better investment opportunities, is obtained by Shah and Thakor (1988). In their first proposition, they state that "*under symmetric information between the founding owner and the manager, the hurdle rate for project acceptance is lower with public incorporation than with private incorporation*". Derivation of this statement is quite intuitive: public sale of equity allows ownership to be shared with well-diversified investors who ignore idiosyncratic risk in pricing the assets. Consequently, although both the owner and the manager are concerned about idiosyncratic risk as a result of their undiversified portfolios in private as well as public firms, the introduction of outside investors in a public firm makes such a firm attach lesser overall importance to idiosyncratic risk than a private firm. The consequence is that projects with relatively high idiosyncratic risk may be rejected by the private firm but accepted by the public firm. In this proposition, they assume that information between the owner and the manager is symmetric in order to isolate the effect of incorporation mode from that of asymmetric information.

Shah and Thakor (1988) also value the choice between public and private financing and its effect on investment policy depending on the degree of information asymmetry between the owner and the management. They demonstrate that in a private firm, asymmetric information between the owner and the manager causes the project's acceptance hurdle rate to rise, therefore causing more projects to be rejected. This results from informational surplus that a manager can extract due to his/her informational advantages. Moreover, the distortion that is caused by information asymmetry increases with the degree of owner's risk aversion.

The intuition is that when the owner is significantly risk averse, he/she finds it optimal to give the manager a higher share of ownership as compensation for reporting to the owner private information, only available to the manager, on the quality of the firm's projects. The owner's behavior stems from optimal risk-sharing considerations. The owner must therefore face a clear trade-off: on the one hand, his/her risk aversion causes him/her to increase the risk sharing with the manager; on the other hand, the higher the fraction of ownership left to the manager in response to private information revelation, the higher the informational surplus the manager can extract will be, therefore increasing the informationally induced distortion in investment policy in terms of hurdle rates. If the firm were publicly held, the increase in the owner's risk aversion would cause no distortion in investment policy because the owner could share the risk with outside investors without any need to increase the share of ownership given to the manager.

The above discussion has a lot of empirical implications for the choice between public and private financing. First, under symmetric information between owner and manager, public ownership always dominates private ownership in terms of optimal set of investments. Second, under asymmetric information between owner and manager, public ownership dominates private ownership in terms of optimal set of investments if listing costs are sufficiently low to offset the informational surplus extraction by the manager. If costs associated with selling shares to outside investors are significantly high, the owner could be induced to increase the share of ownership given to the management, thereby increasing the informationally induced distortion in investment policy. In this case, the owner could opt for private ownership. Public ownership could be more desirable in any case, leading to a better aggregate investment, if the owner is sufficiently risk averse and the firm's assets are sufficiently exposed to idiosyncratic risk.

Third, whenever the owner is better off with public ownership than with private ownership, there is greater investment in the public firm than in the private firm. Finally, for the owner of an initially privately held firm with sufficiently high idiosyncratic risk, going public becomes more desirable (under asymmetric information between the owner and the manager) as his or her prior about the profitability of his or her investment opportunity becomes more favorable. This last statement is important: it suggests that the most productive assets in the economy will tend to be publicly owned and traded.

In conclusion, the following insights can be drawn regarding the relationship between a firm's investment policy and the decision to go private: (1) all other things being equal, listed firms with less productive assets are more likely to go private; (2) all other things being equal, listed firms with sufficiently low idiosyncratic risk (i.e., firms with assets poorly exposed to non-systematic risk) are more likely to go private.

1.4.3 Access to Capital

In terms of capital-based motivations, the purpose of a firm that goes public is twofold: on the one hand, gaining access to new resources otherwise unavailable in the private capital market; on the other hand, raising funds on better terms than those found by the same, privately held firm. These results can be achieved in different ways. First, the proceeds of the public offering can be used to decrease the leverage ratio (Pagano et al. 1998). The expansion of the equity base and the consequent deleveraging help mitigate the debt overhang and other agency problems in the future (Myers 1977). Second, the status of a listed firm increases the number of financing channels available to firm. The listing not only expands the investor base for equity capital, but also makes additional financing forms such as publicly traded bonds, convertible bonds, preferred equity, and other less traditional channels accessible. Third, the improved company image and competition between capital suppliers allow the firm to negotiate bank facilities at more favorable conditions.

The enhanced access to external capital and the reduction of its cost caused by the listing, *ceteris paribus*, should decrease the so-called degree of financial constraint (Fazzari et al. 1988). A firm is considered financially constrained when its investment spending is strongly dependent on the availability of internal funds, rather than just on the availability of positive NPV projects. Accordingly, financially constrained firms are those that have a higher sensitivity of investments to internally generated cash flows.[17] This sensitivity should increase for firms that face larger quantity as well as cost constraints (i.e., quantity constraints are related to the relevance of the credit rationing; cost constraints are related to the wedge between the internal and external costs of funds).

The higher the difference between the cost of internal funds and that of external resources, the lower their degree of substitutability will be. Likewise, the higher the credit rationing, the lower is the degree of substitutability between internal and external funds. Consequently, once a firm has exhausted cheaper internal funds, it has to tap into external finance for the investments to be made.

A financially constrained firm is forced to shrink its investment spending as a result of its poorer ability to use external funds. This means that, for a financially constrained firm, a given cash flow shock is likely to result in a marked change in its investments. In contrast, unconstrained firms should show no investment-cash flow sensitivity because they have access to virtually all external sources of funds. Consequently, a given cash flow shock does not affect investments at all.

The direct implication for the going private choice is that the more the firm is financially constrained, the lower its propensity to go private will be. The reason is straightforward: the access to public equity market is a way of reducing a firm's financial constraints. If a firm already listed faces problems of financial constraint, all other things being equal, these problems are likely to become more severe when the firm opts to go private.

1.4.4 Liquidity

A company's securities are liquid to the extent they can be traded quickly and at low cost. Investors therefore incur the so-called liquidity costs whenever they trade securities. Liquidity costs consist of two components: (1) *direct trading costs*: brokerage commissions, exchange fees, taxes, and so on; (2) *price-impact costs*: potentially far larger, they reflect the price concession, in the form of a premium when buying a stock and a discount when selling a stock, that the buyer or seller must make to effect a trade.

[17] The debate on how to measure a firm's financial constraint was very lively, starting with the pioneering study by Fazzari et al. (1988) and continuing with Kaplan and Zingales (1997), Fazzari et al. (2000) and Kaplan and Zingales (2000) who responded to each other.

For example, when traders and market makers observe a buying pressure, they may suppose that the purchaser has good information on the stock. They will therefore tend either to keep securities in their portfolio or only sell securities to the buyer at a higher price. Likewise, if they observe a selling pressure, they may suppose that bad information is available to the seller who wants to dispose of its securities. They will therefore be inclined to buy stocks only at a lower price.

In both cases, traders and market makers protect themselves by requiring price discounts or premiums that increase with the quantity sold to or bought by them. The price impact will tend to increase with the degree of information asymmetry between buyers and sellers. The greater the potential disparity of information between the trading parties, the greater the risk that the party initiating the trade will take advantage of its counterparty, and the greater the compensation required by the counterparty for doing the trade. In this way, a greater asymmetry of information results in a larger price impact and higher cost of trading.

In addition to information asymmetry, the price impact also depends on the so-called inventory risk. It is caused by the fact that when market makers buy a stock, they need to hold it in inventory until buyers appear. During this period, they face the risk that the price will fall by the time they sell it. If market makers make commitments to sell more shares than they have in inventory, they risk having to cover their positions by buying back the stock at a higher price. Consequently, the greater the asymmetric information and the inventory risk, the wider the bid-ask spread—the difference between the buying and selling prices posted by market makers. For investors, the bid-ask spread represents the market impact of a small trade.

Amihud and Mendelson (1986) made the first effort to demonstrate the existence of a relationship between the liquidity of the company's own stocks and their value and expected return. They assume that investors want to maximize the expected present value of cash flows generated by the securities in portfolio, while taking into account differences in two variables: (1) differences in liquidity costs among securities; (2) differences in their own time horizons.

They demonstrated the following fundamental results. First, the expected return on a stock is an increasing function of its liquidity costs because all investors, regardless of their time horizon, require compensation for bearing these costs. Second, at the same time, this positive relationship between liquidity costs and expected returns is concave. This means that the additional return required for a given increase in liquidity costs should become progressively smaller for incrementally less liquid assets.

The logic underlying this prediction is that less liquid assets tend to be held by investors with longer investment horizons; because such investors effectively amortize their liquidity costs over a longer period, the annualized liquidity costs are lower, and the resulting marginal increase in expected return is smaller as one moves toward increasingly less liquid assets.

Third, in the case of normally highly liquid assets, a sudden and unexpected decrease in liquidity could have much larger price effects precisely because such assets tend to be traded more frequently and thus incur more trading and market-impact costs per annum.

Their analysis therefore suggests that while the return premium for illiquidity is small in the case of more liquid stocks, changes in the liquidity of such stocks have larger effects on their values because they tend to be held by frequent traders who care more about liquidity. The extent that stock prices respond to market-wide liquidity shocks is called liquidity risk.

In sum, the price of a security is affected both by the level of its liquidity (liquidity costs) and by its liquidity risk. Amihud and Mendelson (1986)'s intuition was extended by subsequent studies that on the one hand, demonstrated that stocks whose return is more sensitive to overall liquidity shocks have higher average returns than otherwise comparable stocks with less sensitivity to liquidity (Pástor and Stambaugh 2003), on the other hand, tried to incorporate the liquidity risk in more sophisticated asset pricing models (Acharya and Pedersen 2005).

Which insights can we derive on how the liquidity could affect the choice between public and private financing? First of all, it is quite obvious that going public increases stock liquidity just because the shares start to be publicly traded on the stock market. Despite this clear advantage, a firm may decide to go private, therefore losing the liquidity benefits connected with the floating because of reasons strictly related to the significant reduction in liquidity that a listed firm's stocks may have to bear over time.

If the degree of liquidity goes below critical thresholds, remaining a listed firm may no longer be the optimal choice in the sense that the firm may reach a higher value by delisting its shares from the public market. We therefore need to know the main corporate characteristics that can both enhance and deteriorate the liquidity in order to understand why firms with certain characteristics may choose to go private. Moreover, we will try to identify some actions that firm managers can carry out in order to either preserve or restore a sufficiently high level of liquidity and make the choice to remain a public firm the most profitable one for investors.

The following discussion draws on papers by Amihud and Mendelson (1988, 1991, 2012) on firms that are more likely to benefit from liquidity-enhancing corporate strategies. As is to be expected, the riskier a given stock is, and thus the greater the level of uncertainty about its future value, the greater is the price impact and inventory risk, and the higher the associated liquidity costs tend to be.

Consequently, highly risky firms, such as those operating in high-technology industries, are more likely to have less liquid shares and, ceteris paribus, could find it worthwhile to go private. Similarly, the higher the company's leverage ratio, the greater is the risk of its equity and, as a result, the greater the sensitivity of the value of its equity to new or private information about the firm. Therefore, informed investors have more room to exploit this greater sensitivity to the detriment of market makers and other less informed investors.

The likely result of such information asymmetry is a wider bid-ask spread, higher price-impact costs, and a lower liquidity (Bharath et al. 2009). In other words, market makers and less informed investors protect themselves by increasing the bid-ask spread so as to reduce the risk that informed investors may profit from the increased sensitivity of the market value of equity to new or private information. All other things being equal, highly leveraged firms may find it more convenient to delist their shares from the public market because of their reduced liquidity.

In the same fashion, smaller, informationally opaque firms tend to have shares that are less liquid than those of large, well-known firms as a result of three main factors: first, smaller firms suffer asymmetric information problems to a greater extent than their larger counterparts that have a generally better quality of information disclosure and are followed more closely by the financial press, institutional investors, and analysts. Second, smaller firms have an investor base that is generally smaller (Merton 1987) and their shares are likely to have a smaller float. This is also due to the fact that small firms tend to have more concentrated ownership structures. Third, since the smaller size is related to higher risk and uncertainty over future earnings and cash flows (Fama and French 1995), small firms are less liquid as a result of their higher risk. Consequently, smaller firms, ceteris paribus, could be more induced to go private. In sum, high-risk and informationally opaque firms such as high-technology firms, companies with debt-burdened capital structures, and smaller firms are more likely to go private because of the lower liquidity of their shares.

In addition to lower liquidity, the shares of these firms are also more sensitive to market-wide illiquidity shocks in the sense that when market liquidity falls unexpectedly, the price of these shares experiences a far larger drop than that of other shares, implying an increase in expected returns. The explanation is that when liquidity drops sharply enough, investors generally shift from less liquid to more liquid securities which exacerbates the price decline of these firms, while cushioning the negative effect on large, less risky, and well-known firms.

This is one example of the well-recognized phenomenon known as "flight to quality". Of course, these firms can decide either to remain public because the loss of liquidity is not sufficiently large to exceed other benefits of having publicly traded shares or put in place actions aimed at restoring a level of liquidity that makes the going private choice less appealing. This choice is highly strategic because it directly affects a firm's cost of capital and therefore its value.

First, managers of highly leveraged firms should evaluate the opportunity to reduce the leverage ratio by weighing costs (e.g., lower tax shield, higher agency costs of free cash flow, weaker monitoring of managers, higher managerial entrenchment, etc.) and benefits (e.g., higher liquidity, lower costs of financial distress, etc.) of the choice. The higher liquidity of less leveraged firms is a variable that has to come into play. Besides, there is considerable evidence suggesting that companies can facilitate their access to the market for equity capital by increasing the liquidity of their stocks (e.g., Baker and Stein 2004). To this end, management may want to explore other means of increasing the liquidity of their company's shares.

Another factor that affects a stock's liquidity is the size of its float. This factor has been considered as one of the reasons why a small firm may have a liquidity that is lower than that of a large company. The problem of insufficient float comes into play not only in small firms but also in large firms issuing multiple securities. If a company issues more types of securities, it may be more able to cater to specific contracting needs and the preferences of different investor clienteles. But the downside of this complexity is that with more types of securities, the issue size of each security is smaller which reduces liquidity. In other words, issuing multiple types of securities leads to a fragmentation of a company's investor base and this can reduce liquidity and value.

The implication for managers is that firms with several types of outstanding securities should consider the possibility of either making a unification into a single class so as to expand its float and liquidity or delisting the least liquid classes from the public market. Given that illiquid stocks cannot be converted into cash quickly and cheaply, any corporate strategy that provides investors with the cash they want without the need to trade securities on the stock market is likely to increase firm value.

A means of achieving this goal may be a firm's payout policy. It is well known that in a world without liquidity costs, stockholders can replicate any cash flow stream they desire by trading in the market. This makes dividend policy irrelevant (Miller and Modigliani 1961). But when such trading is costly, this dividend irrelevance proposition no longer holds. The more costly it is to trade in a stock, the greater the potential role of dividends in providing liquidity for the stock's owners. Thus, dividend increases are likely to be most valuable for stocks with low liquidity where the alternative of generating cash flows by selling the stock is more costly. Banerjee et al. (2007) show that firms with less liquid stocks are more inclined to distribute higher amounts of cash dividends.

We can question the ability of many of the least liquid stocks, particularly those with low or negative free cash flow, including small and high-growth companies with large outside funding requirements, to pay out cash dividends. But for those firms with relatively illiquid stock and enough confidence in their future free cash flow to consider paying dividends, an increase in investor liquidity could become a decisive factor that can affect the decision to go private.

Amihud and Li (2006) find that the stock price reaction to announcements of dividend increases is positively related to the illiquidity of the stock. The market reaction is also more positive for stocks with smaller market capitalization, which tend to have higher liquidity costs.

With reference to stock repurchase, the other main means of distributing cash to shareholders, it also appears to affect liquidity which in turn affects corporate decision-making. Since companies incur liquidity costs when buying back their own stocks, stock repurchases are more costly when the firm's shares are relatively illiquid. In addition, if a company is suspected of using private information regarding the firm's prospects when deciding on the timing of a specific stock repurchase, the knowledge that a large trader with private information is in the market may well reduce the liquidity of the stock. For both of these reasons, stock repurchases are likely to be undertaken by companies with relatively liquid stocks (Brockman et al. 2008).

In sum, dividends are more likely to be initiated and increased in companies with less liquid shares. At the same time, the proportion of total corporate distributions made through share buybacks is larger for companies with more liquid stock. The intuition is that dividend increases could be a means in the hands of managers to counter illiquidity problems that could make the going private choice more desirable.

A firm's liquidity can also be improved by enhancing its investor base (Merton 1987), especially by adding small individual investors who trade the stock without private information. Theory suggests that greater trading activity by such less informed investors can have the beneficial effect of reducing the extent of asymmetric information in trading and increasing liquidity, as reflected in the reduction of bid-ask spreads and the price impact of trades. In this way, an increase in a company's number of less informed investors could lead to a higher stock price.

Voluntary disclosure of information is another way to improve liquidity (Amihud and Mendelson 1988; Diamond and Verrecchia 1991). If information on the firm is imperfectly distributed among investors, any effort to increase a firm's transparency in order to convey more information to investors, especially the smallest and the least unsophisticated ones, will decrease information asymmetry, the bid-ask spread, thereby reducing the cost of capital and increasing a firm's liquidity and its value.[18]

This result can be achieved, for example, by making corporate financial statements more transparent (Barth et al. 2013), by releasing earnings guidance and other management forecasts (Coller and Yohn 1997), and by increasing communication with analysts also with the aim of increasing their coverage (Brennan and Subrahmanyam 1995; Roulstone 2003). Firms with poorly liquid stocks should therefore weigh the benefits of voluntarily increasing transparency in terms of improved liquidity, against the costs in terms of potential loss of competitive advantage (Verrecchia 1983, 1990; Yosha 1995). This trade-off is likely to be more significant for companies with high growth opportunities that need to raise capital to fund them, particularly innovative firms that are financially constrained. Such companies, on the one hand, can be expected to find ways of making their stock more liquid in order to reduce the cost of the capital they raise. On the other hand, they could be less inclined to disseminate a lot of (detailed) information about their business in order not to cause undesirable actions by competitors, therefore risking losing their competitive advantage.

How can increased liquidity improve the corporate behavior of listed firms? First, since increased stock liquidity reduces a company's cost of equity, it is also likely to reduce the hurdle rate set by the company when

[18] Empirical evidence on this matter was found by Botosan (1997) and Barth et al. (2013).

evaluating new investment projects. This, in turn, is likely to lead to increased investment and, since the returns are expected to exceed the cost of capital, an increase in corporate values. Second, greater stock liquidity is likely to improve the quality of a firm's corporate governance. Maug (1998) suggests that a more liquid stock increases the willingness of active investors to take large positions in companies and exercise a value-increasing discipline on management.[19] In line with Maug (1998)'s argument, a number of studies in recent years have shown that activist hedge funds are more likely to acquire blocks in companies with more liquid stocks (e.g., Edmans et al. 2013).[20]

Besides, managerial compensation is also found to be affected by stock liquidity. Executives are indeed more willing to have a larger share of equity in their compensation when the firm's equity is more liquid. For one thing, a more liquid stock enables managers to sell their positions at lower cost. But perhaps more importantly, the prices of more liquid stocks are likely to do a better job of reflecting (an insiders' view of) the value of the firm and the contribution of managerial skill and effort to the firm's success (Jayaraman and Milbourn 2011).

Taken together, these findings suggest that greater stock liquidity is associated with more informative stock prices, more active governance by large investors, and greater use of incentive features in managerial compensation. All of this may explain the findings of a study by Fang et al. (2009) which reports that changes in liquidity are positively associated with changes in corporate market-to-book ratios and operating performance.

The messages to managers who are evaluating the possibility of going private are manifold. First, if the firm is small, little known, and does not have particularly highly sensitive information that could jeopardize its competitive advantage should it be disseminated, increasing the quality and the quantity of information voluntarily disclosed could be a good

[19] Bhide (1993) has a different opinion. Most efforts to increase corporate liquidity involve an increase in the number and turnover of shareholders and, in the process, a reduction in the stability and, perhaps most importantly, the concentration of ownership. Bhide (1993) argues that increases in liquidity can weaken corporate governance in underperforming companies by making it easier for dissatisfied investors to sell their shares instead of attempting to bring about constructive change by engaging managements and boards. Coffee (1991) offers a similar thesis and argues that public ownership incurs the high shareholder dispersion that weakens the control on managers that can be carried out better by the private ownership.

[20] The tension between liquidity and corporate control and its effect on the choice between public and private financing will be discussed in greater detail later on in the text.

strategy to improve liquidity, thereby reducing the propensity to go private. Second, managers should avoid increasing a firm's leverage excessively. Highly leveraged firms are less liquid than their less indebted counterparts, therefore reducing the benefits of having shares publicly traded on the stock market. Third, if the firm has reasonably good expectations about its future cash flows, it may initiate or increase cash dividends instead of using share buybacks whenever its shares are or become poorly liquid. This helps to increase the value of the listed firm, therefore reducing the convenience of going private. Fourth, the firm should consider enhancing its investor base by increasing advertising expenditures, improving investor relations, effecting stock splits and stock consolidations (for firms with multiple classes of securities), as well as issuing new shares to new investors. Fifth, the firm should look for and catch as many investment opportunities as possible in order to attract investor attention. Without investment opportunities, the firm is more likely to be disregarded by the investment community and could lack the needed investor base and liquidity. Finally, improving liquidity has also direct implications for investment policy and corporate governance: the former is likely to get better as a result of the lower cost of capital that enhances the value of assets in place and increases the volume of positive NPV projects; the latter is likely to improve as a result of the increased presence of activist institutional shareholders and the greater equity-based share of managers' compensation packages.

1.4.5 Corporate Governance, Control Considerations and the Tension Between Liquidity and Control

Zingales (1995) was the first one to consider corporate control as a factor explaining the decision to go public. His intuition is that the choice to take a company public as well as the decision to go private should be addressed in terms of optimizing the firm's ownership structure in order to maximize the proceeds that the initial owner can obtain by eventually selling his company. Zingales' (1995) insight draws on a game based on three agents that act on a timeline. The agents involve the incumbent (i.e., the initial owner of the firm who has to decide whether or not to go public and the fraction of equity that he wants to retain), the outside shareholders (i.e., beneficiaries of the shares that will be sold in the IPO), and the rival (i.e., a potential buyer, an individual, or a corporation that wants to acquire the firm).

The timing of the game is as follows: first, the incumbent decides whether to go public and, at the same time, decides the size of the equity stake that he does not want to sell to outside shareholders in the IPO. Subsequently, a potential buyer may appear. If it appears, a bargaining phase aimed at negotiating the control of the company starts. The control will therefore be transferred to the buyer depending on the outcome of the bargaining phase.[21] Regardless of the fact that the initial owner gives up the control, the game ends.

However, if the buyer does not appear, the game continues and new information on the characteristics of the potential buyer will be disclosed. The initial owner has therefore another chance to choose his ownership level before a buyer appears. When the buyer appears, the bargaining phase starts. At this stage, the control could have been transferred to the purchaser or not. The firm is then liquidated and the game ends.[22]

The key points of the game are the following: first, the buyer can either increase or decrease the value of the company after the acquisition. Second, the outside shareholders exactly know if the incumbent will have the incentive to sell the company to the potential buyer at the next stage. This means that they value their equity stake based on the expected cash flows that will be produced by the company, either under the control of the buyer if it prevailed during the bargaining phase or under the control of the incumbent if it decided not to relinquish control. Third, cash flows produced by the firm consist of two parts: the first one is observable and verifiable. It is shared in proportion to the size of the equity stake held; the second one is observable but non-verifiable. It is only received by the party who has control of the corporate resources and it is called private benefits of control. This means that this portion of the firm's cash flows is not available to outside shareholders. Let's assume that the components of a firm's cash flows are as follows:

[21] Bear in mind that the bargaining phase has to start if the incumbent, after selling the shares to outside shareholders, still retains control. In contrast, if, after the IPO, he no longer has the majority of votes, the control transfer may occur independently of the incumbent agreement. The buyer, faced with the incumbent rejection of its offer, may launch a tender offer directly to dispersed shareholders. However, Zingales (1995) shows that for the initial owner, relinquishing control is never optimal.

[22] The fact that a company is better sold in stages for considerations related to corporate control is also analyzed in Mello and Parsons (1998) and Stoughton and Zechner (1998).

- υ^I and υ^B are the value of a firm's shared cash flows, assuming that the firm is under the control, respectively, of the incumbent or the buyer;
- B^I and B^B are the value of the private benefits of control, assuming that the firm is under the control, respectively, of the incumbent or the buyer.

Zingales (1995) demonstrates that selling a company by means of an IPO is the value-maximizing decision if two conditions are satisfied: (1) the potential buyer values the company more than the incumbent (i.e., $\upsilon^B + B^B > \upsilon^I + B^I$); (2) the value of shared cash flows under the buyer's control is greater than their value under the incumbent's control (i.e., $\upsilon^B > \upsilon^I$). Both conditions imply that the difference between the buyer's and the incumbent's shared cash flows ($\upsilon^B-\upsilon^I$) should be positive and larger than the difference between the incumbent's and the buyer's private benefits of control (B^I-B^B). The convenience of going public will therefore depend on the cross-sectional distribution of ($\upsilon^B-\upsilon^I$) and (B^I-B^B).

The most important implication is that a company is more likely to go public when the private benefits are relatively less important than the shared cash flows. The same reasoning applies to the decision to go private. The more important the private benefits of control in relation to the value of the shared cash flows, the higher is the probability that a company decides to go private. The conditions under which a listed firm finds it convenient to go private can be written as follows: $\upsilon^B + B^B > \upsilon^I + B^I$ and $\upsilon^B < \upsilon^I$. These conditions boil down to $0 > \upsilon^B-\upsilon^I > -(B^B-B^I)$. Given that the previous inequality may hold if and only if $B^I < B^B$, it follows that if private benefits of control are very small with respect to the value of shared cash flows, the above condition is unlikely to be satisfied. This means that the optimal choice for the firm is to remain public.

In contrast, when private benefits of control are sufficiently large, a potential buyer may have a higher valuation for the entire company but lower shared cash flows. In this case, he may find it optimal to take the firm private. Likewise, if the expectation is that the buyer will reduce the value of shared cash flows relative to their value under the incumbent, then the condition $\upsilon^B < \upsilon^I$ is likely to be satisfied. In this case, it is optimal for the incumbent to buy back the shares and take the company private.

This outcome has some fundamental implications. First, when the economy experiences an increase in the aggregate risk premium, the present value of shared cash flows will decrease, thus lowering the stock prices.

Since the value of private benefits is less sensitive to market conditions (Zingales 1994), this makes the value of private benefits relatively larger than the value of shared cash flows. This helps explain why a lot of firms are delisted through PTP transactions during periods of depressed stock market quotations. This result has not yet been systematically investigated by empirical studies, but some promising evidence seems to have appeared.

For example, in 1973–1974, the stock market suffered a precipitous decline. Consequently, a substantial number of very small public companies were traded at particularly depressed prices. The managers of many of these companies, which had recently gone public in the 1960s, still owned controlling or even majority stock interests. But the public market had lost its appeal and many of these owner-managers chose to reverse the public offering of a few years earlier and to return to the quiet life of a private company (Lowenstein 1985).

Likewise, after the 1987 stock market crash, PTP transactions reached a historical peak in 1988. When the Internet bubble burst at the end of 2000, a lot of high-technology firms that survived the collapse decided to go private in the following year(s). This evidence could lead us to think that an IPO clustering-like phenomenon (e.g., Ritter 1984) could also exist in PTP transactions. Indirect support of the above result is found by Brau et al. (2003) and Mitchell and Mulherin (1996). They show an increase in M&A activity during industry or economic contractions. Given that M&As are one of the most common ways to take the firm private, this anecdotal evidence suggests that IPOs and takeovers occur in waves that are negatively correlated as indicated by Zingales (1995). Second, PTP transactions, ceteris paribus, should be more likely in countries characterized by poor corporate governance quality, poor minority shareholder protection and, consequently, high private benefits of control.

However, the model proposed by Zingales (1995) ignores the fact that control considerations are likely to interact with other motivations underlying the decision to go either public or private. Other studies (e.g., Bhide 1993; Coffee 1991; Bolton and Von Thadden 1998; Maug 1998; Pagano and Röell 1998) indeed show that control dimensions trade-off against liquidity issues in the sense that, on the one hand, a public firm benefits from a higher liquidity of its shares that ceteris paribus leads to a higher value of the company. A higher liquidity can be achieved, among other things, by expanding investor participation which is typically larger in firms with higher ownership dispersion. On the other hand, high ownership dispersion may give rise to ineffective monitoring of managers due to free riding by small dispersed shareholders. This could make the creation of controlling blocks that increase ownership concentration desirable at the expense of liquidity.

A lot of theoretical models focus on how liquidity (distinguishing benefit of a public firm) and ownership concentration (typical benefit of a privately held firm) can optimally be traded off against each other in order to maximize firm value. Boot et al. (2008) place into unified framework liquidity considerations, control considerations, and investor participation as simultaneously determined variables by explaining why a firm may decide to go private. The following discussion summarizes the main points of the Boot et al. (2008) model. Their model tries to show the conditions under which private ownership is more desirable than public ownership (and vice versa) for an all-equity publicly traded firm that has to decide whether to go private or remain public in expectation of a growth opportunity. The model flows according to the following timeline:

Timing
t=0

- The firm has assets in place that will produce, at $t = 4$, a non-stochastic cash flow of $S > 0$.
- A coalition of investors may try to take the public firm private by buying all the publicly traded shares; if the coalition fails to take the firm private, the firm continues to be publicly held.
- Once the choice between public and private ownership is made, the firm chooses its governance structure. The choice is made by private investors if the firm is taken private and delisted, otherwise it will be made by outside shareholders.
- The choice of the governance structure, in turn, implies the determination of the level of the so-called managerial autonomy. Managerial autonomy is the extent to which managers may decide on the realization of the project (i.e., the growth opportunity) in the event of disagreement with investors (i.e., investors may disagree with managers over the profitability of the project. This means that managers may want to carry out the project while investors may not and vice versa. Managerial autonomy is a measure of the extent to which the managers' decision prevails over the investors' decision).

$t=1$

- Managers can expend privately costly *search efforts* to find the project that will become available with probability e at $t = 3$. The manager's private cost of search effort is $\frac{\beta e^2}{2}$ where $\beta > 0$ is a constant.

$t=2$

- Liquidity needs by investors show up and need to be satisfied by trading some assets.

$t=3$

- Managers and investors learn about project availability and draw their prior beliefs about its quality. Disagreement between managers and investors over project quality may occur.

$t=4$

- The project will generate cash flows.

The Choice Regarding Project Implementation and Resolution of a Potential Disagreement Between Managers and Investors

Depending on project availability at $t = 3$, managers and investors draw on their prior beliefs about project quality at $t = 3$. Project quality can be "good" (G) or "Bad" (B). If the project is G-type, the level of its cash flows, in turn, depends on the so-called managerial preparation effort ε. Preparation effort includes activities such as feasibility studies and other costly commitments related to the evaluation of the project realization. If managers expend ε at $t = 3$, they incur a personal cost of $\psi > 0$. With preparation effort, the G-type project will increase the firm's cash flows from S to X_G. Without preparation effort, the project will not affect cash flows and it will therefore remain at level S. Regardless of the preparation effort, the B-type project will reduce the firm's cash flows from S to 0. In sum, the *search effort*, at $t = 1$, will affect the probability of project availability at $t = 3$. Conditional on the project being available at $t = 3$, the *preparation effort* will affect the profitability of the G-type project.

Now we need to formalize the prior beliefs of managers and investors about the project quality. Let θ_m represent the managers' prior beliefs about the probability that the project is G-type. Let us also assume that $\theta_m \in \{\theta_l, \theta_h\}$,[23] with $\theta_l < \theta_h$. Let $\delta \in \{0, 1\}$ be the probability of managers

[23] θ_l and θ_h can be seen as, respectively, "low" prior beliefs (a sort of worst-case scenario) and "high" prior beliefs (a sort of best-case scenario), conditional on the appearance of a G-type project.

drawing θ_h and $1 - \delta$ be the probability of managers drawing θ_l. This means that the managers' perception of the project value depends on their prior beliefs θ_m ***and*** the preparation effort choice. We can therefore define $X_h = \theta_h X_G + [1 - \theta_h]0 = \theta_h X_G$ and $X_l = \theta_l X_G + [1 - \theta_l]0 = \theta_l X_G$ as the perceived values of the project when managers expend preparation effort ***and*** their prior beliefs are θ_h and θ_l, respectively. We also assume that $X_l < S < X_h$. This implies that the project has a positive NPV, conditional on the preparation effort, when the prior belief is θ_h. In contrast, the project has a negative NPV when the prior belief is θ_l; this happens regardless of the preparation effort. Consequently, managers will not expend any preparation effort whenever their prior beliefs about the project quality are θ_l. In this case, the project's perceived value by managers is just $\theta_l S + [1 - \theta_l]0 = \theta_l S < S$ and the managers will therefore reject it.

With reference to the prior beliefs of investors about the project quality, the approach is of the kind just seen. Let θ_i represent the investors' prior beliefs that the project is G-type, where $\theta_i \in \{\theta_l, \theta_h\}$. Agreement between managers and investors about the desirability of the project occurs when $\theta_i = \theta_m$ with probability ρ. Disagreement occurs when $\theta_i \neq \theta_m$ with probability $1 - \rho$. This means that ρ represents the probability that managers and investors have a common prior belief about project quality. The greater the value of ρ, the higher the likelihood of agreement between managers and investors will be; $\rho = 1$ indicates perfect agreement, while $\rho = 0$ indicates perfect disagreement.

The agreement parameter ρ can be thought of as being affected by the attributes of the project (i.e., the nature of the firm's business), the length of the time series of relevant historical data (i.e., the age of the firm), the managers' previous track record in managing similar projects of that type, and possibly also the general level of investor confidence in the corporate sector.

If the project is one that managers have previously dealt successfully with for a long time and investors are familiar with it as well, ρ will tend to be high. Since project familiarity and confidence in the managers' prior track record can be expected to vary in the cross-section of investors, there can be heterogeneity among investors in the extent of their agreement with managers, even when all investors and managers have rational beliefs.

In case of agreement between investors and managers, the decision about the project is transparent: if both the managers and the investors draw a prior belief of θ_l, managers do not expend preparation effort and they agree to eschew the project since they both perceive a negative NPV of $\theta_l S - S$. Similarly, if both the managers and the investors draw a prior belief of θ_h, the managers expend preparation effort and there is mutual agreement to undertake the project with a positive NPV of $X_h - S$. Disagreement may arise when prior beliefs differ. If managers draw θ_l, then they will not expend preparation effort, ε, and will perceive project value as $\theta_l S$. If, in this case, investors draw a prior belief of θ_h, investors will anticipate that managers will not expend preparation effort; they will therefore perceive project value as $\theta_h S < S$,[24] and they will also want to avoid the project. However, when the managers' prior belief is θ_h, they will expend preparation effort and will wish to implement the project,[25] provided that the cost ψ is not prohibitive, but investors will wish to reject the project if their prior belief is θ_l.[26] This is the key disagreement we focus on.

Investor Participation, Agreement, and Firm Value

Heterogeneity among investors in the extent of their agreement ρ with managers can be modeled by assuming that public market is formed of N investors and that the ρ for each investor at any point in time is an independent draw from a continuous probability distribution $G(\rho)$, with the associated density function $g(\rho)$ and support $[\rho_l, \rho_h]$. Whenever a project decision has to be made, the investors holding the firm's shares in the public market are the ones who have the highest level of agreement with the managers (hereafter "maximal investors") among the cross-section of investors; this is because they assign the highest value to the firm and can thus outbid all other investors in a competitive capital market.[27]

[24] Bear in mind that without preparation effort, the project will not affect the firm's cash flows which will remain at level S.

[25] In this case, the project has a positive NPV of $X_h - S$.

[26] In this case, for investors, the project has a negative NPV of $\theta_l X_G - S$.

[27] This implies that the higher the level of agreement with managers, the higher the value of the company for investors will be. This point will be demonstrated later on. However, intuitively, this result arises from the fact that when there is agreement, the value that investors attach to the project will be $X_h = \theta_h X_G$ (if the prior belief is θ_h) or $\theta_l S$ (if the prior belief is θ_l). Vice versa, in case of disagreement, the value for investors will be $\theta_h S$ (if the prior belief is θ_h for investors and θ_l for managers) or $\theta_l X_G = X_l$ (if the prior belief is θ_l for investors and θ_h for managers). In the event of agreement, managers and investors always agree in making the project or not and there is one scenario in which the project has a positive NPV for investors. In case of disagreement, the project has always a negative NPV for investors and in one scenario (when the managers' prior belief is θ_h), the managers, according to their managerial autonomy, may decide to implement it despite investors not wanting it. This means that, ceteris paribus, the value of the company for investors is increasing in the level of agreement ρ.

We assume that the investors with the highest ρ have collectively sufficient wealth to own all the shares of the firm, that is, all the investors holding a firm's shares have the same ρ. Thus, although there is heterogeneity among public-market investors, for a particular firm, there is homogeneity in the identity of its actual investors, in terms of their agreement with the managers.

Liquidity Needs and Costs

With probability one, investors require cash at $t = 2$ in order to satisfy a liquidity need at that time. Investors have two alternative ways of meeting their liquidity need. They can either sell some illiquid asset in their portfolio other than their shares in the firm, or they can sell their shares in the firm. If investors choose to sell some other illiquid asset, a liquidity cost of $L > 0$ is incurred by the seller. If investors choose instead to sell their shares in the firm, the cost depends on whether the firm is public or private.

Let's assume we have an investor in a public firm. If the investor decides to sell his shares at $t = 2$ in response to a liquidity need, then public listing of the firm's shares ensures that the transaction occurs in a well-defined market that has active, low-cost trading, with the market price at any point reflecting the valuation of the maximal investors. At $t = 2$, the investor thus assesses the valuation of the firm at $t = 3$ as being dependent on $\bar{\rho}$, the expected value, assessed at $t = 2$, of the ρ of the maximal investor at $t = 3$; we will prove formally later on that the share sale price at $t = 2$ will be increasing in $\bar{\rho}$.

Moreover, selling at $t = 2$ in a liquid public market will involve no search cost in finding a buyer, and the investor can thus sell his shares without any delay or significant cost. The only possible cost such an investor may perceive is that his own ρ may be higher than $\bar{\rho}$, in which case he is selling his shares at a price lower than his own valuation. The investor will however choose to sell his shares if the perceived cost of doing so is less than L, the liquidity cost of selling some other illiquid asset. The sufficient condition that guarantees this is that the price discount stemming from selling shares to other investors when $\rho > \bar{\rho}$ is lower than L. Put differently, as long as L is sufficiently large, public investors will be willing to sell their shares even at a discount.

An important consequence of such trading is that it creates uncertainty about the identity of future shareholders and hence about ρ. Since the project selection decision is taken at $t = 3$, it is only the ρ at that point in time that matters. The ρ at $t = 3$ is the ρ of the maximal investor who buys shares at $t = 2$, because there is no further liquidity trading after $t = 2$. At $t = 0$, the managers are uncertain about this ρ because at $t = 2$, the existing investors in the firm's shares exit due to liquidity need-based trading.

By contrast, private ownership lacks an analogous market transaction mechanism. Hence, when private investors wish to sell shares, finding a buyer involves costly and time-consuming search, which costs $c > 0$. Such a search results in finding an investor who represents only a random draw from the cross-section of potential buyers, with an expected agreement with the managers that equals the mean of the distribution of all ρ's in the cross-section, that is, $E(\rho)$. This contrasts with the competitive market-clearing mechanism that continuously reflects the valuation of the marginal investor in the case of the public market.

Private investors will retain the firm's shares and incur the liquidity cost L in selling some other illiquid asset if the sum of the search cost c and the loss (gain) from selling to a buyer with an "average valuation" is greater than L. We will assume this to be the case for all private investors. The condition that ensures private investors to hold their shares is that $c > L$. If c is sufficiently large, private investors choose not to sell. The private investors thus retain their ownership in the firm, implying that the relative illiquidity of private ownership results in an unchanged identity of the initially identified investors.

Managerial Autonomy

Managerial autonomy intends to provide a rule that settles the disagreement between managers and investors over project choice that occurs when managers want to invest but investors do not. Disagreement is resolved by determining the probability with which the managers get to decide and the probability with which the investors decide. This can be thought of as a bargaining game in which there is some probability that managers move first and make a take-it-or-leave-it offer to the investors and some probability that the investors get to move first. If the take-it-or-leave-it offer is rejected, the firm comes to a standstill and managers as well as investors get a payoff of zero. The probability with which the managers move first is called managerial autonomy $\eta \in [0, 1]$. Because the first mover in this game has all the bargaining power, η is the probability with which the managers will invest in the project when the investors disagree with them; $1 - \eta$ is the probability that investors will stop the managers from investing in this state. η can be meant as a sort of corporate governance parameter that specifies the degree of control given to the managers: the lower the η, the higher the stringency of the governance will be (i.e., lower autonomy).

Ceteris paribus, the managers prefer more autonomy to less. This is not because they have an innate preference for control, but because greater autonomy gives them greater ability to maximize their assessment of *security benefits*, that is, the value of cash flows generated by the project.[28] The level of managerial autonomy η is endogenously determined (following the choice between public or private ownership) at $t = 0$, after which the managers simply take η as fixed for their subsequent decisions.

Under either ownership mode, the optimal η is set by investors to maximize the share price. The managerial share ownership α is taken as exogenously fixed. Any optimal contract, designed to provide effort incentives for managers, will involve a nonzero managerial ownership stake. Given a positive managerial ownership stake, autonomy becomes relevant to the managers because they perceive the value of their ownership to be increasing in managerial autonomy.

Once the variables and the timing that come into play have been stated, we need to formulate the relationships among these variables, their determinants, and their impact on the decision to go private. The analysis is performed by using backward induction, i.e., we start at $t = 4$ and go back to $t = 0$. Since no decision is made at $t = 4$, we go back to events at $t = 3$ and examine them for both public and private ownership. $t = 3$ when managers and investors learn whether the growth opportunity is available and also whether they agree on pursuing it.

This is based on the expected agreement between managers and investors which is ρ_{pr} for the private firm and $\overline{\rho}$ for the public firm. We examine how these are determined and the managers' choice of preparation effort, ε. We then move to $t = 2$. This is when investors experience a liquidity need; we examine the behavior of both public and private investors in response to this need. Next, we examine the managers' choice of search effort, e, at $t = 1$, under both public and private ownership. Finally, we examine how managerial autonomy is determined under public and private ownership at $t = 0$ and how the firm makes its ownership choice at that time.

[28] The positive relationship between managerial autonomy and the perceived value of the ownership stake held by managers will be demonstrated later on.

t = 3, Determination of Level of Agreement and Preparation Effort

We know that managers will expend preparation effort ε after they draw a prior belief of θ_h that the project is G-type and has been accepted. For any other prior belief, the managers reject the project and the issue of investing in the preparation effort is therefore irrelevant.

Level of Agreement with Public Ownership ($\bar{\rho}$)

When the project implementation decision is made at t = 3, the firm's shares will be held by the investors with the highest agreement with managers. This is because, for a given level of managerial autonomy in the public market, such investors will have the maximum valuation for the firm's shares and should be able to outbid all others.[29] Thus, $\bar{\rho}$ is the expected agreement of the maximal investor with managers. When ρ varies cross-sectionally and the ρ for any investor is a random draw from a probability distribution, the highest value of ρ among the N investors—the ρ of the maximal investor—is the Nth-order statistic of ρ, say ρ_N, where

$$\rho_N = \max_{1 \le i \le N} \{\rho_i\}.$$

According to the standard properties of the Nth-order statistic, we have:

$$\bar{\rho} = \frac{N!}{(N-1)!} \int_{\rho_l}^{\rho_h} G(\rho_N)^{N-1} g(\rho_N) \rho_N d\rho_N.$$

It follows that:

1. the expected value of ρ_N, $\bar{\rho}$, is increasing in N;
2. the variance of ρ_N, σ_N^2, is decreasing in N.

The reason behind the previous result is that the greater the number of investors in the market, N, the higher will be the agreement parameter of the maximal investor, ρ_N, since there are more investors to choose from. Thus, $\bar{\rho}$ is increasing in N. Similarly, the greater the number of participat-

[29] See also the discussion in section "*Investor participation, agreement and firm value*" for the motivations behind this result.

ing investors, the smaller the variance in the agreement of the maximal investor will be. This result highlights two important effects of higher investor participation. The first is an increase in the expected value, $\bar{\rho}$, of the agreement parameter, ρ_N, and the second is a reduction in its variance. Because there is a one-to-one relationship between the expected value of ρ_N and the level of the stock price with public ownership and also between the volatility of ρ_N and the volatility of the stock price, this result implies that the level of the stock price will increase and its volatility will diminish as investor participation increases. Black (1976) indeed empirically documents a negative relationship between stock returns and volatility typically explained in terms of lower corporate leverage ratios with rising stock prices. This intuition gets to the same result without depending on corporate leverage.

Level of Agreement with Private Ownership (ρ_{pr})
ρ_{pr} will be derived as an endogenous variable when the firm's choice of whether to continue with public ownership or go private will be examined.

t = 2, Investors' Liquidity Needs

Given the conditions already stated (see section "Liquidity needs and costs"), investors in public firms face liquidity needs by selling their shares; investors in private firms face liquidity needs by selling some other illiquid asset and incurring a cost L, while holding the firm's shares.

t = 1, Managers' Optimal Choice of Search Effort

Public Ownership
The managers' choice of search effort e at $t = 1$ takes as a given the degree of autonomy under the public ownership, η_{pub}, determined at $t = 0$, and maximizes V^M_{pub}, that is, their expected payoff, which is given by:

$$V^M_{pub} = E\begin{pmatrix} \alpha\left\{e\delta\bar{\rho}\left[X_h - S\right] + e\delta\left[1-\bar{\rho}\right]\eta_{pub}\left[X_h - S\right] + S\right\} \\ -e\delta\left\{\bar{\rho} + \left[1-\bar{\rho}\right]\eta_{pub}\right\}\psi - \dfrac{\beta e^2}{2} \end{pmatrix}$$

$$= E\left(\alpha W^M_{pub} - e\delta\left\{\bar{\rho} + \left[1-\bar{\rho}\right]\eta_{pub}\right\}\psi - \frac{\beta e^2}{2}\right)$$

Where $W^M_{pub} = \{e\delta\bar{\rho}[X_h - S] + e\delta[1-\bar{\rho}]\eta_{pub}[X_h - S] + S\}$ is the managers' assessment of the firm's value at time $t = 1$.

In more detail, the first term of W^M_{pub}, that is, $e\delta\bar{\rho}[X_h - S]$, is the increase in the firm's cash flows when there is a project that occurs with probability e, and both managers and investors have the same prior belief θ_h, that occurs with probability $\delta\bar{\rho}$. The managers will expend preparation effort and the project will therefore be implemented with a positive NPV. The second term, that is, $e\delta[1-\bar{\rho}]\eta_{pub}[X_h - S]$, is the increase in the firm's cash flows when there is a project that occurs with probability e, and managers have a prior belief of θ_h but investors draw a prior belief of θ_l, that occurs with probability $\delta(1-\bar{\rho})$. In this case, managers will be able to undertake the project only with probability η_{pub} as a result of the disagreement with investors. The last term, that is, S, is the cash flow from assets in place because in all states other than those reflected in the first two terms of W^M_{pub}, the project has a negative NPV and will therefore be rejected with the consequence that the firm's cash flow will remain at level S. The remaining terms of V^M_{pub}, that is, $\left(-e\delta\{\bar{\rho}+[1-\bar{\rho}]\eta_{pub}\}\psi\right)$ and $\left(-\frac{\beta e^2}{2}\right)$ represent the private costs borne by managers in, respectively, preparation effort ψ, that occurs with probability $e\delta\{\bar{\rho}+[1-\bar{\rho}]\eta_{pub}\}$, and search effort.

The probability associated with preparation effort $e\delta\{\bar{\rho}+[1-\bar{\rho}]\eta_{pub}\}$ is the product of the following probabilities representing the likelihood that managers undertake this effort: (1) probability that a project appears (without a project, no preparation effort will be carried out), e; (2) probability of managers drawing a prior belief of θ_h (without a prior belief of θ_h, there will be no preparation effort), δ; (3) probability that investors accept the managers' investment choice, $\bar{\rho}+[1-\bar{\rho}]\eta_{pub}$. This is the sum of the probability of having an agreement between managers and investors about project quality and the probability of not having an agreement multiplied by the probability that managers' decision prevails over investors' choice.

The managers' uniquely optimal choice of effort level under public ownership is as follows:

$$e^*_{pub} = \frac{\delta}{\beta}\left[\{\bar{\rho}+[1-\bar{\rho}]\eta_{pub}\}\{\alpha[X_h - S]-\psi\}\right]$$

Where e^*_{pub} is strictly increasing in: (1) the expected level of agreement, $\bar{\rho}$; (2) the managerial autonomy, η_{pub}; (3) the fraction of managerial ownership, α.

These results are intuitive. The higher the expected level of agreement between managers and investors, the higher the probability that the project will be implemented will be. This implies greater returns for managers' effort. The same reasoning applies to managerial autonomy. With reference to the fraction of managerial ownership, the higher the managerial ownership, the higher the incentive of managers to expend effort will be, because their wealth is positively influenced by the greater value of their stake following the implementation of the project that in turn, will be more likely in response to higher levels of agreement and autonomy parameters.

Private Ownership

V^M_{pr} and W^M_{pr} can be derived in the same identical way as seen for V^M_{pub} and W^M_{pub} and have the same meaning, but substituting $\bar{\rho}$ and η_{pub} with, respectively, ρ_{pr} and η_{pr}, which are agreement and autonomy parameters in the event of private ownership. Therefore, we will have:

$$V^M_{pr} = E\begin{pmatrix} \alpha\left\{e\delta\rho_{pr}\left[X_h - S\right] + e\delta\left[1-\rho_{pr}\right]\eta_{pr}\left[X_h - S\right] + S\right\} \\ -e\delta\left\{\rho_{pr} + \left[1-\rho_{pr}\right]\eta_{pr}\right\}\psi - \dfrac{\beta e^2}{2} \end{pmatrix}$$

$$= E\left(\alpha W^M_{pr} - e\delta\left\{\rho_{pr} + \left[1-\rho_{pr}\right]\eta_{pr}\right\}\psi - \frac{\beta e^2}{2}\right).$$

Where $W^M_{pr} = \left\{e\delta\rho_{pr}\left[X_h - S\right] + e\delta\left[1-\rho_{pr}\right]\eta_{pr}\left[X_h - S\right] + S\right\}$.

Likewise, the managers' uniquely optimal choice of effort level under private ownership is as follows:

$$e^*_{pr} = \frac{\delta}{\beta}\left[\left\{\rho_{pr} + \left[1-\rho_{pr}\right]\eta_{pr}\right\}\left\{\alpha\left[X_h - S\right] - \psi\right\}\right]$$

Where e^*_{pr} is strictly increasing in: (1) the expected level of agreement, ρ_{pr}; (2) the managerial autonomy, η_{pr}; (3) the fraction of managerial ownership, α.

$t = 0$, Choice of Managerial Autonomy Under Public (η_{pub}) and Private Ownership (η_{pr})

We first determine the optimal level of managerial autonomy under public ownership, η^*_{pub}, and then the optimal level of managerial autonomy under private ownership, η^*_{pr}.

Public Ownership

The optimal level of managerial autonomy is determined by outside investors at $t = 0$ in order to maximize their expected payoff, V^I_{pub}, taking into account the impact of this choice on the managers' subsequent choice of optimal search effort, e^*_{pub}. Investors therefore maximize:

$$\begin{aligned} V^I_{pub} &= E\left(\left[1-\alpha\right]\left\{e^*_{pub}\delta\bar{\rho}\left[X_h - S\right] + e^*_{pub}\delta\left[1-\bar{\rho}\right]\eta_{pub}\left[X_l - S\right] + S\right\}\right) \\ &= E\left(\left[1-\alpha\right]W^I_{pub}\right) \end{aligned}$$

Where $W^I_{pub} = \left\{e^*_{pub}\delta\bar{\rho}\left[X_h - S\right] + e^*_{pub}\delta\left[1-\bar{\rho}\right]\eta_{pub}\left[X_l - S\right] + S\right\}$ is the investors' assessment of the value of the firm at $t = 0$. If we compare W^I_{pub} with W^M_{pub}, the key difference between the two expressions is that, in the second term, which shows the increase in the firm's cash flow when managers and investors disagree about the project implementation (i.e., managers have a prior belief of θ_h but investors draw a prior belief of θ_l), investors value the project's NPV as $X_l - S < 0$, while managers value it as $X_h - S > 0$. This also implies that investors' evaluation of the firm's value increases with the level of agreement between managers and investors, $\bar{\rho}$. This result confirms the previous conclusion (see footnote 27). The optimal level of managerial autonomy under public ownership can be derived as follows:

$$\eta^*_{pub} = \frac{\bar{\rho}\left[X_h + X_l - 2S\right]}{2\left[1-\bar{\rho}\right]\left[S - X_l\right]} \in (0,1).$$

Where η^*_{pub} is increasing in $\bar{\rho}$ and the project cash flow (X_h or X_l).

This result establishes the characteristics of the governance regime under public ownership. First, managerial autonomy is increasing in the level of agreement. The reason is that the greater the propensity of investors to agree with managers, the lower the "cost" of granting autonomy to the managers will be. In other words, higher agreement implies lower probability that managers behave differently from investors. Consequently, giving higher autonomy to managers is less "dangerous" for investors. Second, managerial autonomy also increases along with the attractiveness of the growth opportunity (X_h or X_l). In this case too, the result is straightforward: the greater the (X_h or X_l), the lower the "cost" of managerial autonomy will be. The "cost", in terms of lower firm value that investors would bear in the event of disagreement decreases as the quality of growth opportunity increases. This extends the result provided by Boot et al. (2006), where η^*_{pub} is an exogenous variable. η^*_{pub} in the present model is endogenously determined because we want to analyze the impact of investor participation on public governance arrangements.

Trying to find a thread among the variables discussed above, the following relationships can be drawn.

Higher levels of investor participation in the public capital market, N, lead to:

1. lower values of the variance of the agreement parameter ρ_N;
2. higher levels of $\bar{\rho}$, the expected value of the agreement parameter ρ_N that, in turn, lead to
3. higher values of the optimal public-market managerial autonomy level, η^*_{pub}, and
4. higher values of V^M_{pub}, the expected value of managers' payoff with public ownership.

It follows that greater investor participation in the equity market results in corporate governance that grants more decision-making autonomy to management. The reason is that greater investor participation leads, on average, to higher agreement between managers and investors, paving the way for greater autonomy for managers. If firms with more analyst coverage (i.e., the larger and better-known firms) can be viewed as those with greater investor participation, then this result says that the larger and better-known firms will optimally have less stringent corporate governance as represented by greater managerial autonomy. Moreover, these firms with greater autonomy will also have lower stock price volatility.

This outcome was unintentionally tested by Gompers et al. (2003). They infer from the values of their governance index that managers in larger firms enjoy greater takeover protection. Assuming that takeover protection is a reliable proxy for greater managerial autonomy, the insights provided by Boot et al. (2008) are confirmed. Moreover, greater investor participation in the public equity market makes public ownership more attractive. This is intuitive. Greater investor participation increases the probability of finding investors with higher levels of agreement with managers and hence induces higher valuations. This also implies that security benefits are endogenized via a managerial autonomy-contingent "investor approval" process that affects the expected value of security benefits for managers.

The flip side of this is that low levels of investor participation will reduce the valuations of public firms and this may provide a possible explanation for some empirical observations of relatively small firms that complain about having received inadequate attention from security analysts and investors that have begun to go private; the large number of Internet and high-tech firms that went private after the bust of Internet bubble; the growth of delisted firms, that did not file for bankruptcy, in the aftermath of the subprime mortgage financial crisis occurred in 2008–2009 and the subsequent European sovereign-debt crisis, started in 2010, especially in the stock exchanges of the most affected European countries such as Italy,[30] Spain, and so on and in the second markets, such as the UK AIM (Alternative Investment Market),[31] mostly dedicated to hosting small, less-established firms.

Private Ownership

If the firm goes private, then at $t = 0$, the level of managerial autonomy, η^*_{pr}, is set to maximize the expected payoff of private investors given as follows:

$$\begin{aligned} V^I_{pr} &= E\left(\left[1-\alpha\right]\left\{e^*_{pr}\delta\rho_{pr}\left[X_h - S\right] + e^*_{pr}\delta\left[1-\rho_{pr}\right]\eta_{pr}\left[X_l - S\right] + S\right\} - L\right) \\ &= E\left(\left[1-\alpha\right]W^I_{pr} - L\right) \end{aligned}$$

Where $W^I_{pr} = \left\{e^*_{pr}\delta\rho_{pr}\left[X_h - S\right] + e^*_{pr}\delta\left[1-\rho_{pr}\right]\eta_{pr}\left[X_l - S\right] + S\right\}$ is the investors' valuation of the firm at $t = 0$. W^I_{pr} expression is similar to that for W^I_{pub} with the difference that in the former the agreement and autonomy parameters are, respectively, ρ_{pr} and η_{pr}, while in the latter these parameters take the form of $\overline{\rho}$ and η_{pub}. It is worth noticing that the private investors' level of

[30] Pagni, L., 2012. "Edison e le altre cinquanta. La grande fuga da Piazza Affari. Così la crisi ha rivoluzionato il listino della Borsa", *La Repubblica*, August 18. Monti, M., 2012. "Ex quotate. La bufera sui mercati ha incrementato il numero di uscite dalla Borsa negli ultimi quattro anni. La crisi e quei 50 "addii" a Piazza Affari", *Il Sole 24 Ore*, February 2.

[31] Stothard, M., 2012. "Economic woes lead to AIM delistings", *Financial Times*, January 3.

agreement, ρ_{pr}, could be different from the expected level of agreement, $\bar{\rho}$, since investors experience a liquidity need before the project shows up and incur a liquidity cost of L with probability one (see also footnote 32).

The optimal managerial autonomy under the private ownership is as follows:

$$\eta_{pr}^{*} = \frac{\delta \rho_{pr}\left[X_h + X_l - 2S\right]}{2\delta\left[1-\rho_{pr}\right]\left[S - X_l\right]} \in (0,1)$$

Where η_{pr}^{*} is increasing in ρ_{pr} and the project cash flow (X_h or X_l).

An important insight of the above discussion is that public-market corporate governance is more rigid than private corporate governance $\left(\eta_{pub}^{*} < \eta_{pr}^{*}\right)$. This is because η_{pub}^{*} is set based on the expected value, $\bar{\rho}$, whereas the private-ownership autonomy parameter, η_{pr}^{*}, is based on the realized ρ. Given that private investors incur a liquidity penalty of L (they have to sell some other illiquid asset at $t = 2$ to meet liquidity needs), for the private ownership to be valuable to investors, at least as the public one, they must have a relatively high level of agreement with managers, ρ_{pr}, that, in turn, implies a higher level of autonomy parameter, η_{pr}. Consequently, the private ownership model would imply greater agreement and autonomy and therefore more lax corporate governance.

The Choice Between Public and Private Ownership at $t = 0$

At $t = 0$, for a coalition of investors with the maximal valuation for the firm's shares to prefer to take the firm private, their valuation of the private firm should exceed the share price with continued public ownership. This is also a necessary condition for a going-private transaction to succeed. Once the condition under which private ownership is the preferred option has been stated, we need to know the variables that affect the choice. Drawing on the above discussion, it is possible to find a cutoff value, $\hat{\rho}$, of the agreement parameter, ρ_{pr}, with $\hat{\rho} > \bar{\rho}$,[32] such that private investors with $\rho_{pr} > \hat{\rho}$ will strictly prefer to take the firm private. This implies that the higher the value of $\hat{\rho}$, the lower the probability of going private will be. The following relationships can therefore be inferred.

[32] The inequality $\hat{\rho} > \bar{\rho}$ holds because of L, the liquidity cost under private ownership. In fact L reduces the private investors' valuation of the company under private ownership (V_{pr}^{I}). This implies that for the private ownership to be preferred, the cutoff value of ρ_{pr} should be greater than $\bar{\rho}$, the expected level of agreement in the public market, and, in turn, the inequality $\rho_{pr} > \hat{\rho} > \bar{\rho}$ should hold.

The cutoff value $\hat{\rho}$ increases (i.e., the probability of going private decreases) with.

1. the expected level of agreement in the public market, $\overline{\rho}$;
2. the liquidity cost of private ownership, L;
3. the cash flow without the project, S;
4. the level of investor participation in the public market, N.

The cutoff value $\hat{\rho}$ decreases (i.e., the probability of going private increases) with

5. the variance of the agreement parameter, σ_N^2;
6. the cash flow with the project, X_h or X_l.

First, a higher level of agreement between managers and investors in the public market, that is, $\overline{\rho}$, leads to a higher value of the publicly held firm for investors. This reduces the probability that investors find it profitable to take the firm private. Moreover, since the investors' perception of firm value under private ownership increases with the extent of agreement with managers the extent of agreement with managers, ρ_{pr}, then only private investors with a relatively high level of agreement with managers will be able to pay a sufficiently high price to take the firm private. In fact, since $\rho_{pr} > \hat{\rho} > \overline{\rho}$ has to hold for the private ownership to be desirable and firm value is strictly increasing in ρ, the prediction holds that going-private transactions will occur only at significant premium over the pre-announcement stock price.

Second, given that investors under private ownership, at $t = 2$, incur a liquidity penalty of L because they have to sell some other illiquid asset while retaining their shares, a greater value of L makes private ownership less attractive.

Third, for the private ownership to be chosen, it has to be $\rho_{pr} > \hat{\rho} > \overline{\rho}$. This implies that the agreement between managers and investors under private ownership should be greater than their agreement under public ownership. This, in turn, implies higher managerial autonomy and greater probability of implementing the project under private ownership.[33] In other words, public ownership is characterized by a lower probability that the project will be carried out therefore the cash flow generated by the growth opportunity is

[33] Bear in mind that $\rho_{pr} > \overline{\rho}$ leads to higher managerial autonomy and greater level of managerial effort which, in turn, give rise to higher probability of project implementation under private ownership.

relatively less important than the cash flow produced by the assets in place. It follows that higher cash flows from assets in place, *S*, make public ownership more desirable and hence reduce the probability of going private.

Fourth, it has already been shown that greater investor participation positively affects the level of agreement in the public market, $\bar{\rho}$, and, by means of this, it makes private ownership less appealing.

Fifth, given that higher value of the variance of the agreement parameter, σ_N^2, corresponds to higher stock price volatility, this higher volatility on the public market increases the attractiveness of private ownership.

Sixth, we have shown (see point 3) that public ownership is more desirable than the private one when the cash flow from assets in place, *S*, is greater because the public ownership implies lower probability of carrying out the project therefore making the quality of growth opportunity relatively less important than the quality of existing assets. Likewise, reversing the statement, private ownership leads to higher probability for the project to be implemented. Consequently, cash flows with the growth opportunity, X_h or X_l, become relatively more important under private ownership therefore their greater value makes private ownership more likely.

Predictions of the Model and Testable Empirical Implications: A Summary

The model proposed by Boot et al. (2008) is very comprehensive in its aim to link many of the most important aspects that affect the decision to go private. It also offers a battery of testable predictions, some of them already tested in other empirical papers, but either without providing a formal explanation of the evidence or providing motivations unrelated to those suggested by Boot et al. (2008). In what follows, we provide a summary of these predictions and their testable dimension.

1. Higher *investor participation* makes public ownership more desirable. Greater investor participation leads to higher agreement in the public market between managers and investors which, in turn, implies a higher value of the public firm for investors. The testable prediction is that we should observe higher frequency of IPOs in bull markets and higher frequency of PTP transactions in bear markets. The first phenomenon has been observed extensively by the advocates of the market timing theory in explaining IPOs (Ibbotson and Jaffe 1975; Ritter 1984; Lucas and McDonald 1990; Loughran et al. 1994; Pagano et al. 1998; Lowry 2003; Ritter and Welch 2002). The second phenomenon, so far, has found some (indirect)

confirmation (e.g., Brau et al. 2003; Bharath and Dittmar 2010) and a number of empirical regularities (e.g., 1988 peak of PTP transactions after the stock market crash in 1987; the large number of firms, especially those belonging to the new economy, that went private after the end of the dot-com bubble in 2000; the rising number of firms that chose the private ownership after the financial crisis triggered by the collapse of the US subprime mortgage market in 2007–2008) seem to support this prediction.

Moreover, given that firm size, analyst coverage, and the level of institutional ownership are good proxies for investor participation, Bharath and Dittmar (2010) show that consistent with the investor participation hypothesis, firms having greater analyst following and those with higher share of institutional investors in their ownership structure are less likely to go private. In contrast, the size of the firm does not produce consistent results: larger firms, that should be better-known, are found to have a higher probability to go private. Mehran and Peristiani (2010) find the same evidence as Bharath and Dittmar (2010) except the firm size. They indeed find smaller firms to be more inclined to go private as prescribed by Boot et al. (2008).

2. The price paid by investors to buy all the outstanding publicly traded shares should incorporate a significant *premium* over the price at which those shares were traded on the public market before the bid. This is because only private investors with a relatively high level of agreement with managers will be able to pay a sufficiently high price to take the firm private so as to satisfy the condition $\rho_{pr} > \hat{\rho} > \bar{\rho}$. This prediction was confirmed by a large number of studies that focused on the shareholder wealth effects of PTP transactions and leveraged buyouts (e.g., DeAngelo et al. 1984; Kaplan 1989a, b; Lehn and Poulsen 1989 and, more recently, Guo et al. 2011).
3. Since $\rho_{pr} > \hat{\rho} > \bar{\rho}$, it follows that managerial search effort is also higher if the firm is taken private than if it continues to be public. Consequently, this implies a higher firm value with private ownership, generating the prediction that a public firm that goes private should exhibit improved performance and be worth more *after* going private.[34] Evidence consistent with this prediction was found, for example, by Kaplan (1989a), Smith (1990) and Guo et al. (2011).

[34] Bear in mind that the managers' total payoff under private ownership (V_{pr}^{M}) increases in managerial search effort, e, which, in turn, increases in the degree of agreement under private ownership, ρ_{pr}.

4. PTP transactions are more likely when the firm's cash flows from assets in place, *S*, are ***low*** and when cash flows with the growth opportunity, X_h or X_l, are ***high***. This prediction is not consistent with a principal-agent model with private benefits of control which argues that PTP transactions are more beneficial to shareholders when the firm generates abundant cash flows and does not have significant growth opportunities. In this scenario, the improved monitoring provided by the private ownership should reduce agency costs arising from the conflict between managers and shareholders (Jensen and Meckling 1976; Jensen 1986).

   This prediction is not even supported by most empirical studies. Bharath and Dittmar (2010) show that, before the 1990s, the free cash flow hypothesis is supported in the sense that firms with higher free cash flows are more likely to go private. After the 1990s, the free cash flow hypothesis seems to have become unimportant in affecting the decision to go private.[35] They also show that firms with lower market-to-book ratio which proxies for a firm's growth opportunities are more likely to go private. This result too is not consistent with Boot et al. (2008).
5. When the ***stock price volatility increases***, publicly held firms are more likely to go private. This prediction was tested by Mehran and Peristiani (2010) and Kashefi Pour and Lasfer (2013) who found inconsistent results with Boot et al. (2008). Mehran and Peristiani (2010) found a negative relationship between volatility and probability to go private. They explain this by relying on the fact that the low volatility may be characteristic of cash-rich firms, with few growth opportunities, unable to attract interest from investors, but that could be a suitable target for leveraged buyouts. Moreover, the result is consistent with the financial distress hypothesis proposed by Opler and Titman (1993) according to which distressed firms, being more risky, are less likely to be the target of leveraged buyouts. Kashefi Pour and Lasfer (2013) found statistically insignificant results.
6. Public firms characterized by ***high managerial autonomy*** are less likely to go private. This is a consequence of the higher investor participation and the higher agreement between managers and

[35] See also Lehn and Poulsen (1989), Denis (1992), Opler and Titman (1993) and Mehran and Peristiani (2010) for evidence that is consistent with the free cash flow hypothesis. Vice versa, Maupin et al. (1984), Kieschnick (1989, 1998) and Servaes (1994) show different results.

investors under public ownership. The testable prediction is as follows: assuming that managers who are insulated from the risk of being replaced through takeover are more likely to enjoy higher managerial autonomy, greater managerial entrenchment should be associated with a lower probability that a firm goes private.[36]

Gompers et al. (2003) find that larger firms' managers seem to enjoy higher protection against takeover threats. This implies that larger firms are less likely to go private. This evidence is found in Mehran and Peristiani (2010) and Kashefi Pour and Lasfer (2013). Bharath and Dittmar (2010) find opposite results.

However, public firms with higher insider ownership too are less likely to be threatened by takeover, leading to higher managerial autonomy. We should therefore find a lower probability to go private in firms with higher insider ownership. Mehran and Peristiani (2010) and Kashefi Pour and Lasfer (2013) find evidence that does not support the prediction proposed by Boot et al. (2008). A possible explanation is that insider ownership, above a certain level, exacerbates the conflict between managers and shareholders and reduces the attractiveness of public ownership by using an approach based on the relevance of private benefits of control (e.g., Zingales 1995). Put differently, an excessively high level of insider ownership could lead investors to evaluate private benefits of control as being large. Consequently, they are more inclined to be in control in the event of disagreement with managers. This implies a lower level of $\bar{\rho}$ as well as a lower desirability of public ownership.

7. A private investor with a sufficiently high level of ρ_{pr} should appear for a firm to be taken private. It follows that the larger the number of potentially interested private investors, the larger the probability that any one of them may bid for taking the public firm private. In other words, a larger pool of investors specialized in private equity implies a higher probability that a firm may come across one of them with a level of ρ_{pr} large enough to take it private. The testable prediction is that the development of the private equity market should increase the intensity of PTP transactions. Empirical evidence seems to support the prediction (Acharya et al. 2007; Bharath and Dittmar 2010).

[36] For example, Bebchuk et al. (2009) propose five clauses (i.e., staggered boards, limits to amend by-laws, supermajority requirements for mergers and charter amendments, poison pills, and golden parachutes) which should provide a measure of the degree of managerial entrenchment. Consequently, firms that meet these provisions are less likely to go private according to Boot et al. (2008).

8. The probability of a going-private transaction declines as the liquidity cost of private ownership, L, increases. One way to test this would be to compare going-private transactions across markets or countries that have private equity markets with varying levels of liquidity. Some empirical evidence (Strömberg 2007) finds that leveraged buyouts undertaken in Continental Europe are less likely to leave private ownership than those carried out in the US and the UK.

   On the one hand, the greater longevity of LBOs in Continental Europe may prove that private investors face a lower value of L. On the other hand, the higher holding period in Continental Europe could also be due to higher cost of search effort, c, expended to find a convenient exit way (i.e., a buyer). Given the relatively lower level of liquidity of exit markets in Continental Europe, the second explanation is more likely to hold. This could help explain why PTP transactions are more common in the US and the UK. However, this does not seem to be due to a lower value of L.
9. *Ceteris paribus*, the higher the price paid to take the firm private, the less stringent the corporate governance put in place *after* the firm is taken private. This follows from the fact that managerial autonomy under private ownership increases with ρ_{pr}, and from the fact that the higher the value of ρ_{pr}, the higher is the private investors' valuation of the firm.
10. In a way that may appear counterintuitive, it is the very liquidity of the public market that prevents a publicly held firm from being able to get managers to expend a level of search effort that is as high as that of managers in a privately held firm. The role of private ownership is to inhibit any sale of shares by the private investors which ensures investor stability and relatively high managerial search effort.

    This role cannot be duplicated by a liquid public market. In fact, the private investors hold on to the firm's shares until $t = 3$. This provides stability to the agreement between managers and investors which facilitates better matching between η_{pr} and ρ_{pr}, and ensures a higher level of managerial effort. This stability cannot be assured under the public ownership model. In fact, even if an investor with $\rho = \rho_{pr}$ bought all the outstanding publicly traded shares at $t = 0$, fixed the level of managerial autonomy to maximize its valuation, and was committed not to sell shares until $t = 3$, managers in the public market would anticipate the fact that the investor would incur a liquidity need at $t = 2$, after managers have expended the research effort at $t = 1$. By anticipating this sale, managers will not expend the optimal search effort.

The higher rigidity of corporate governance in publicly held firms goes hand in hand with lower managerial search effort.[37] This also shows a trade-off between liquidity and control: greater liquidity assured by the public market implies lower managerial control (i.e., autonomy). Since shareholder base instability under public ownership induces a lower managerial effort, instruments aimed at hampering ownership turnover such as lock-up agreements, the presence of multiple classes of shares,[38] and a bonus share offered to IPO investors that hold shares in their portfolio for at least a specified number of months after the IPO, and so on could enhance ownership stability and reduce the downside of the public ownership.

Model Extensions: The Impact of Firm Age on the Decision to Go Private

Older firms generally have a longer track record of project implementation and a reasonably higher correlation between their new projects and their past successful projects. These intertemporal connections across projects allow managers and investors to learn about project returns and potentially reduce the heterogeneity of beliefs between them. This means that firms with a history of project implementation are more likely to experience belief convergence. It follows that the learning process by managers and investors regarding project implementation may affect the manager-investor agreement in different stages of a firm's life which, in turn, may affect its ownership choice depending on the firm's age.

Let's assume that the firms can be of two types, "*old*" or "*young*" and that they have access to incremental projects every period. Project payoffs are uncertain and the managers and investors have heterogeneous prior beliefs about project payoffs. As before, the investors who hold the firm's shares are those with beliefs closest to those of the managers, or equally, the highest level of agreement with the managers. Every period, the managers and the investors observe a common signal about the project but may disagree over the optimal implementation decision. Conditional on this disagreement, the managers are in control with probability η. Let's indicate with

[37] In fact, for private ownership to be desirable, it has to be $\rho_{pr} > \hat{\rho} > \bar{\rho}$. Given that managerial autonomy is increasing in ρ and managerial search effort is increasing in ρ and η, it follows that managerial search effort under public ownership will be lower than that under private ownership.

[38] Voting shares are generally held by managers and the largest shareholders. They should therefore be less affected by trading activity. This, in turn, could further be limited by transfer restrictions that often accompany voting shares held by insiders.

r the probability that an old firm's incremental project is a repeat project that the firm has successfully implemented in the past and with $1 - r$ the probability that the incremental project is a completely new project without any history. In contrast, for the young firm, the incremental project is completely new with probability one.

Prior to the nature of the project being revealed, the expected agreement between the managers of an old firm and investors is equal to $\rho_{old} = r\rho_r + [1 - r]\rho_n$, where ρ_r is the agreement for a repeat project and ρ_n is the agreement for a new project. For a young firm, the agreement is equal to $\rho_{young} = \rho_n$. The agreement for an old firm, ρ_{old}, will be greater than the agreement for a young firm, ρ_{young}, if $r\rho_r + [1 - r]\,\rho_n > \rho_n$ or $\rho_r > \rho_n$. This inequality says that the expected agreement will be greater for an old firm if the agreement for a repeat project, ρ_r, is greater than that for a new project, ρ_n.

In order to provide an intuitive demonstration that $\rho_r > \rho_n$ is always satisfied under certain conditions, in the sense that an old firm with a successful repeat project will have a higher agreement with investors than a young firm, let's assume that the managers' prior belief about the expected project payoffs is $N(\mu^M, \sigma^2)$ and the investor i's prior belief is $N(\mu^i, \sigma^2)$. Without loss of generality, we also assume that the managers and the investors have the same belief about the variance of the expected payoffs. In the cross-section of investors, the μ^is are random draws from a continuous distribution with support $[0, \mu^M]$. Therefore, the managers' prior mean represents the maximum possible prior mean of the investors. This is plausible because the managers are likely to choose the projects they are most bullish about. This ensures that the managers always have a higher prior knowledge about the expected project payoffs than the investors and that the agreement between the managers and the investors is increasing in the mean of the investors' prior beliefs.

Given these assumptions, Boot et al. (2008) demonstrate that $\rho_r > \rho_n$ holds. The intuition behind this result is that a project success, that is, a high realized payoff, increases both the managers' and the investors' posterior mean of the project payoff. But since the investors' prior mean μ^i is below the managers' prior mean μ^M, the investors' posterior belief exhibits a larger response to a project success. This reduces the gap between the beliefs of the managers and the investors and increases agreement, leading to $\rho_r > \rho_n$. Consequently, managers of an old firm with a successful repeat project will have a higher level of agreement with investors than those of a young firm.

So far, the effect of *N*, that is, the level of investor participation in the public market, is taken as fixed. However, this assumption is unrealistic because *N* may change over time for various reasons, including changes in transaction costs for trading, improved regulation, and so on. Consequently, we need to take into account the effect of *N* on the level of agreement between managers and investors conditional on having a young or old firm. Intuitively, an increase in *N* increases the prior beliefs of the investors with the maximal mean and hence the agreement between the managers and the investors. This is straightforward: the higher the level of investor participation *N*, the higher the probability of finding the maximal investors with a prior mean about the project payoff closest to that of managers. We are then interested in evaluating the impact of this increase in the investors' prior belief on their posterior beliefs. It can be demonstrated intuitively that the impact will be lower for a successful repeat project than for a new project because the realized payoff on the repeat project dampens the impact of the prior. Given that the probability to carry out a new project is higher in a young firm than in an old firm, a change in *N* will have a greater impact on agreement between managers and investors for young firms.

The main implication for the decision to go private is that the elevated sensitivity of young firms toward investor participation implies that these firms will switch between private and public ownership more often. In other words, an increase in *N* will have a bigger impact on the preference of young firms for either remaining private or going public. Similarly, a decrease in *N* will induce young public firms more strongly toward private ownership. Empirical evidence seems to support this prediction. For example, Fink et al. (2010) show that the average age of firms going public in the US declined from 40 years in the 1960s to less than 5 years in the 1990s. This was a period during which public-market investor participation increased significantly, pushing many young firms to go public. Further evidence can be found in international comparisons. Pagano et al. (1998) document that the average age for Italian companies that went public during the period 1982–1991 was 33.43 years, compared with a US average age of about 7 years for venture-backed firms and about 11 years for non-venture-backed firms (Lerner 1994; Gompers 1996).

This result is consistent with Boot et al. (2008) since investor participation in Italian stock market is far lower than that in the US stock market; the presence of a venture capitalist at IPO stage, in turn, can make investor participation even higher. Furthermore, this could help explain, on the one hand, why many young firms went public during the Internet boom of the late 1990s and, on the other, the recent anecdotal evidence that shows a seemingly disproportionately high number of young firms that decide to go private after having been listed on the stock market during the dot-com bubble.

1.4.6 Listing Requirements and Costs

We have shown that the lower the obstacles and costs that an investor has to bear in order to collect information on the firm, the higher the attractiveness of public financing will be in terms of higher liquidity, lower cost of capital, higher diversification, and so on. However, we have also shown that an excessively high level of public dissemination of information may jeopardize the firm's competitive advantage because it may trigger detrimental actions by the firm's competitors. In this section, we will try to examine more closely how the increase in information dissemination and in the cost of going (and remaining) public can affect the choice between public and private ownership.

A modification of listing requirements is one of the most common exogenous actions that can affect the burden a listed firm has to bear in order to continue to be quoted on the stock market. The change can be related to a wide set of factors such as minimum floating, stock exchange fees, the quality of certification, auditing, and dissemination of accounting information, the minimum level of market capitalization, and so on. One of the most influencing factors is changes in the amount and quality of information to disclose to investors. This may happen, for example, when the stock market authorities and/or the government put into effect reforms that make information disclosure requirements more stringent, therefore imposing a higher level of transparency on listed firms.

A wide stream of literature focused on the costs and benefits of the passage of the Sarbanes-Oxley Act of 2002 (SOX). SOX was the legislative response to a series of financial scandals and bankruptcies involving a significant number of US corporations such as Enron, Xerox, Worldcom, and so on that were threatening investors' confidence in the capital markets. The Act was intended to restore this confidence by introducing a large and complex system of provisions involving most participants in a firm's life such as officers, directors, auditing firms, control systems, disclosure rules, and so on. (Coates 2007).

Many parties judged the regulatory burden to be excessively heavy, especially with reference to disclosure rules, internal control systems, and auditor-client relationships. In this respect, SOX requires CEOs and CFOs to certify firms' financial reports and demands more timely and extensive financial disclosures. Companies must disclose transactions on a "rapid and current" basis and provide more detail regarding off-balance-sheet transactions and special purpose entities. Second, SOX requires all public companies to establish and maintain an internal control system for financial reporting and requires management to evaluate the effectiveness of these systems in their annual reports. In addition, external auditors of the company must attest to the management's evaluation. Third, SOX sets more stringent standards for internal audit committee membership. All members of the internal audit committee must be independent and firms must disclose whether at least one member is a financial expert. Fourth, SOX affects the ability of corporate insiders to earn profits from trades of the firms' shares. CEOs and CFOs must disgorge bonuses and stock-sale profits during any twelve-month period following a financial report that is subsequently restated due to misconduct. Furthermore, executives must report insider trades within two days, rather than within ten days following the end of the month in which the transaction occurred. Finally, the Act defines some new criminal offenses and increases criminal penalties attached to existing offenses. New offenses are related to the destruction of documents with intent to obstruct justice. Executives who knowingly certify false financial reports are subject to a fine of $5 million, a 20-year prison term, or both. Criminal penalties are increased for mail fraud, violation of ERISA reporting and disclosure rules, and violation of the Securities Exchange Act of 1934.

In addition to direct costs (i.e., compliance costs, auditing fees, etc.), SOX also led to indirect costs such as opportunity cost of managers' time spent or greater risk aversion as a result of perceived pressure for tighter financial controls (Coates 2007). Although these costs are even harder to measure, they seem to be falling over time, perhaps even more rapidly than direct costs, as the initial managerial attention needed to comply with SOX returns to normal business activities and the degree to which the law increases liability risk becomes better-known. In sum, SOX created new incentives for firms to spend additional money on internal controls, disclosure, auditing, and so on.

In exchange for these increased costs, SOX promises a variety of long-term benefits. Investors will face a lower risk of losses from fraud and theft[39]; benefits will arise from more reliable financial reporting, greater transparency, and accountability.[40] A firm that commits to disclosure mitigates the

[39] Coates (2007) documents a dramatic fall, after the enactment of SOX, of the number of securities frauds alleged in significant class action lawsuits against US public companies.

[40] Coates (2007) documents that earnings management fell after SOX. The correlation that existed before the SOX between abnormal accounting accruals—that is, accruals not

potential for differential informedness among traders, thus reducing the liquidity premium its shareholders expect to pay when they sell their shares; disclosure may reduce management's ability to consume agency goods (i.e., shirking or perquisites) at the expense of shareholders, therefore lowering agency problems arising from the separation of ownership and control. Restrictions on insider trading can benefit shareholders in much the same way. Such restrictions potentially limit liquidity premium and can limit management's incentive to take inefficient actions in order to maintain high share prices in the short run. Ultimately, public companies will pay a lower cost of capital and the economy will benefit because of a better allocation of resources and faster growth. However, the law's full costs are hard to quantify and the benefits even harder. This created a fruitful area of enquiry aimed at estimating the economic consequences of SOX enactment.

The framework described above puts forward some implications for the firms that have to decide whether to remain public or go private. Put differently, SOX may reverse the cost-benefit trade-off of public versus private financing. We can therefore draw a number of testable implications. According to Engel et al. (2007), going-private transactions that are made in response to SOX allow firms to increase their value if the SOX-imposed costs to the firm exceed the SOX-induced benefits to shareholders and this difference overwhelms the net benefit of being a public firm prior to the passage of SOX.

Thus, one would expect the post-SOX going-private firms to be those where (1) SOX compliance costs are relatively high, (2) SOX-related benefits to shareholders are small, and (3) net benefits to being public are relatively small prior to the passage of SOX. Formally, the influence of SOX on the choice between public and private financing can be modeled as follows[41]:

(a) let $V_{i,public}^{pre-SOX}$ be the value of the firm i before the passage of SOX;

predicted by standard empirical models of accruals—and the importance of an audit client to its auditor vanished after the law was passed. Investor confidence also increased after the passage of SOX. Bid-ask spreads and market depth, which were widening and falling, respectively, during 2001–2002, reflecting falling investor confidence, began to tighten and rise again in both the month and in the nine months after the legislation was passed.

[41] Some firms, in order to escape the increased regulatory burden of SOX, go dark instead of going private. The difference is that when going dark, the firm's shares continue to be traded on the Pink Sheets but the firm legally ceases to file SEC disclosures because the number of its shareholders has fallen below the trigger level for SEC registration, while when going private, the firm's shares cease trading. In both cases, companies will no longer be subject to the requirements of SOX. We will go back to this difference later on.

(b) let $V_{i,private}$ be the value of the firm *i* whether it were private in the pre-SOX period. This quantity is surely lower than $V_{i,public}^{pre-SOX}$ because we are assuming that the firm *i* is always public before the passage of SOX. This implies that the benefits of public financing vis-à-vis private financing are higher than the related costs in the pre-SOX period;

(c) let b_i and c_i be, respectively, the benefits and costs of SOX for the firm *i*.

It is value-maximizing for the firm *i* to go private in the post-SOX period if:

$$c_i > b_i + \left(V_{i,public}^{pre-SOX} - V_{i,private}\right)$$

The inequality above will be satisfied depending on the interplay of the three factors (i.e., c_i, b_i, $V_{i,public}^{pre-SOX} - V_{i,private}$). With reference to the first variable, many authors have pointed out that SOX compliance costs are likely to have a significant fixed component which suggests its effects will be more negative for small companies (e.g., Holmstrom and Kaplan 2003). This implies that a relatively large number of small firms are expected to go private in response to the enactment of SOX.

With reference to the second variable, Holmstrom and Kaplan (2003) argue that shareholders of firms that were well governed prior to SOX are unlikely to receive significant SOX-related benefits and thus the costs may exceed the benefits for these firms. Consequently, well managed firms are more likely to go private after SOX. Likewise, since some SOX provisions were directed at making insiders' shareholding less liquid so as to mitigate outside shareholders' concerns of inequitable profit opportunities for insiders, the benefits stemming from more illiquid insiders' equity stakes are expected to be smaller in firms where insiders' holdings were relatively illiquid prior to the passage of the Act.

Moreover, insiders with very high ownership bear most of the cost of consuming agency goods such as perquisites or shirking. Because they bear most of the cost, they consume fewer agency goods and thus their firms may not benefit from a reduction in agency costs as a result of SOX. Large ownership stakes are also relatively more illiquid than small equity holdings. As a result, firms with higher and relatively illiquid insider ownership are more likely to go private after the passage of SOX.

Finally, since the net benefits from being public are relatively smaller for small firms, firms with a limited need for external funding, and firms that are thinly traded, we expect these firms to go private with a higher probability in response to SOX. This may help explain why the collapse of the technology boom in 2001 could have caused many small and young firms to go private: small caps were adversely affected by the collapse of the Internet bubble which made the issuance of new equity more expensive for these companies while simultaneously reducing the trading volume in their stocks. The benefits of being public to many of these small firms may have disappeared when they experienced falling stock prices, reduced liquidity, minimal analyst coverage, and lower trading volume. Consequently, the passage of SOX could have made the costs of being a public firm undeniably larger than its benefits so as to induce many small firms to delist.

Another implication of SOX enactment is the supposed reduction of attractiveness of US stock markets compared with other trading venues. The advocates of this theory claim that SOX has hurt the ability of US stock exchanges (principally the New York Stock Exchange) to compete successfully with foreign stock exchanges (principally the London Stock Exchange) for new listings in general and for cross-listings of foreign firms in particular. This expectation does not appear to have gained empirical support because the decline in the US exchanges' share of cross-listings has been larger in 2001, prior to SOX, than it has been since SOX, and this pattern holds true for high-tech and non-high-tech firms alike (Coates 2007).[42]

Some studies (Bushee and Leuz 2005; Leuz 2007; Engel et al. 2007; Kamar et al. 2009) have focused on the trade-off between costs and benefits of these reforms by analyzing their impact on a firm's decision to stop public trading. The main assumption under investigation is that if the costs stemming from stricter regulation exceed its benefits, ceteris paribus, we should observe a greater number of firms going private after the implementation of such reforms. Kamar et al. (2009) confirm that after SOX, there was a significant growth in the propensity of small public targets listed in the US stock markets to be acquired by private firms and this growth is found to be significantly higher than in Western Europe. This trend is not found in large public firms. Engel et al. (2007) focus on abnormal returns to SOX-passage-related events and find that they are significantly more

[42] Zingales (2007) and Halling et al. (2008) empirically show that US stock markets have been facing increased competition for trading volume from domestic markets, but the trend does not seem to be linked to SOX enactment.

negative for smaller firms and those less actively traded, confirming that the passage of SOX is supposed to be more negative for small and illiquid firms. Moreover, they find that the abnormal return to the announcement of PTP transactions in the post-SOX period is higher than in the pre-SOX period for small firms with higher insider ownership.

1.4.7 Stock Market Myopia and Short-Termism

Graham et al. (2005) surveyed and interviewed more than 400 US executives about the factors that drive reported earnings and disclosure decisions. They found that 78% of the surveyed executives would give up economic value in exchange for smooth earnings. Many executives feel they are choosing the lesser evil by sacrificing long-term value to avoid short-term turmoil in terms of severe market overreactions to earnings misses. The executives believe that less predictable earnings—as reflected in a missed earnings target or volatile earnings—require a risk premium in the market. This behavior of managers, well known as short-termism,[43] is largely triggered by an excessive focus of market analysts, traders, fund managers, and others on quarterly earnings and other short-term metrics. This market myopia may harm the interests of shareholdings seeking long-term value growth and sustainable earnings; if managers and boards pursue strategies simply to satisfy short-term investors such as funds, day traders, and so on, they may put a firm's future at risk.

More formally, the model proposed by Stein (1989) shows that in a market characterized by information asymmetry, in the sense that the firm's managers typically have better information than the market, even supposedly perfectly rational managers are cornered into myopic behavior. The key problem is that if short-run earnings are poor, the market is unable to determine whether this is caused by poor management or by prudent long-term investments, resulting in underinvestment. The market partly uses current earnings to forecast future earnings and knowing this, managers attempt to manipulate the information available to shareholders by increasing current earnings, potentially at the expense of long-term investments, resulting in underinvestment.

[43]According to Demirag (2015), short-termism includes those factors acting upon (or within) an organization which tend to cause decision-makers (a) to raise the discount rate above the cost of capital; and/or (b) to contract the forecast horizon beyond which future revenues are ignored altogether. Such pressures will tend to reduce the rate of investment and/or bias it toward short-term projects.

The key implication of the models based on stock market myopia is that the capital market's obsession with meeting short-term expectations, coupled with asymmetric information problems, may stop corporate managers from focusing on long-term value creation. Consequently, given that public market myopia does not allow managers to take into account economic value in the best interest of a firm's long-term shareholders, executives can decide to go private in order to avoid the market pressure on short-term targets and focus on forward-looking investment plans aimed at creating value in the long-run.

Therefore, we can draw at least a couple of implications for the decision to go private. First, if private firms/managers are less myopic than public firms/managers because of the absence of pressure from public markets, then episodes of going private transactions should cause firms and their establishments to improve their productivity compared with a not-going-private peer group (Bharath et al. 2014). The enhanced productivity should derive from managers being free to invest in long-term, more efficient investments, without any concern to meet short-term market expectations.

Second, the likelihood to go private due to myopia-driven motivations as well as the economic consequences of the following PTP transaction should be higher for firms more affected by short-termism and asymmetric information problems. This means that small firms and firms with more opaque, highly unpredictable earnings suffer market myopia to a greater extent than large, established firms in the sense that they are more committed to earnings management as well as more concerned about short-term performance metrics in order to avoid the market overreaction stemming from a failure to hit earnings target. On the other hand, large and established firms tend to show smoother earnings (Leuz et al. 2003), therefore making the issue of market myopia manageable without resorting heavily to earnings management strategies.[44]

[44] However, Shleifer and Vishny (1997) in their review of corporate governance conclude that the theories and arguments in favor of the view that US companies are relatively short sighted are remarkably short of empirical support. Anecdotal evidence comes from corporate executives who increasingly often state the excessive level of public market pressure to be the main reason for their choice to take the firm private. For example, in 2010, Burger King agreed to a $3.3 billion sale to 3G Capital. 3G Capital took the firm private and its executives and analysts said going private would free Burger King to make major changes without the distraction of pleasing Wall Street (Baertlein, L., 2010. "Burger King agrees to $3.3 billion sale to 3G Capital", *Reuters*, September 2). Likewise, in 2010, Burlington Northern Santa Fe (BNSF) prepared to delist from the public markets following its takeover by Warren

1.4.8 The Use of Derivatives

The huge spreading of derivatives among firms in the last decades may have decreased the attractiveness of public ownership as a result of the reduction of the risk-sharing benefits stemming from being a listed firm (Masulis and Thomas 2009). Based on this motivation, Merton (1995) claims that one of the most important benefits of being public is risk sharing. Since private owners internalize parts of the firm's risks which are diversifiable with widespread ownership, they gain by shifting this risk more broadly.

Another key benefit of being public is access to public capital markets to support firm investment and expansion. As a private firm, expansion is limited by the firm's inability to fund all its projects with added debt, since the default rate on the debt is a positive function of a firm's assets' total risk (return variability) and its leverage (debt-to-asset ratio). Since the demand for equity of privately held firms has generally been quite limited by demands for large price discounts, raising equity capital by private firms has generally been a very expensive option.

Merton (1995) therefore proposes the following hypothetical scenario: let's consider a firm with needs for funding and risk sharing that believes it must move to the public-ownership domain with all its costs that reflect what the firm gives up by going public. To what extent can the firm obtain the benefits of public ownership while preserving the benefits of private ownership? If the firm could hedge these risks, that is, the risks related to the internalization of part of diversifiable risks, then it could reduce the total variation or riskiness of the business, without negatively impacting its profitability. This will reduce the gains from risk sharing and likely lower the future need to raise equity capital.

Buffet's Berkshire Hathaway in a deal valued at $44 billion. Matthew Rose, chief executive of Burlington Northern Santa Fe, said it could be frustrating dealing with quarterly earnings announcements when the company's investments were far longer term and criticized the market's excessive focus on short-term results and the lack of a long-term perspective (Wright, R., 2010. "BNSF chief hits at short-termism", *Financial Times*, February 12). Market pressure is advanced as motivation to go private also outside the US. For example, Ferretti spa, world leader in the production of luxury yachts, chose to leave the Italian stock market in 2003. Ferretti's CEO, Norberto Ferretti, said that the company had to invest €250 million in plants and acquisitions and needed to raise capital. The firm would not have been able to pursue that strategy effectively if the market had been short sighted, not very patient, and excessively punitive toward those firms performing long-term expansion plans (Puato, A., 2002. "Quei titoli perduti", *Il Corriere della Sera*, October 7).

Merton (1995) therefore argues that as hedging becomes widespread, one may well observe a macro shift back toward greater private ownership of firms as these hedging tools are developed and refined. Given the tremendous growth in derivative markets since the 1990s, the relative benefits of public ownership as a means of risk sharing and lowering the cost of capital seem to have declined significantly.

1.4.9 Takeover Defense

A public company that appears to be vulnerable to takeover threats may choose to set up antitakeover defenses to allow managers to preserve their position. Going private is the defense of last resort against a hostile takeover and is effected when the bidder (e.g., a private equity firm or the target firm's managers) wants to obtain or maintain control of the firm (Lowenstein 1985; Shleifer and Vishny 1988). This removes the possibility of an undesired bidder obtaining a controlling position in the firm without the target company management's approval. This motive seems to be more likely in MBOs with large management representation on boards and, to a lower extent, in LBOs.

However, this type of reaction to takeover pressure generally represents a weak motivation to account for the decision to go private; it was largely advocated in the LBO wave of the 1980s. Indeed, many companies that went private through buyouts were often taken public again shortly afterwards and, at least in some cases, their management lost control at that point. Examples of this strategy are reverse LBOs which occur when a company goes private in an LBO only to be taken public again at a later date (e.g., Muscarella and Vetsuypens 1990).

More recently, this motivation regained popularity in a "revised version" as a result of the increased shareholder activism, especially by hedge funds, that threatens target firm managers who may seek to take their firms private to retain control over them (Brav et al. 2008). This motivation is consistent with observed evidence suggesting that hedge fund attempts at interventions frequently lead to private equity buyouts at targeted firms, especially at small- and medium-sized firms.

1.4.10 Agency Considerations and Leveraged Buyout

Most of the motivations to go private we have shown in the previous sections are drawn from reversing the theories of going public in the sense that the decision to go private is explained by resorting to the loss of the net benefit of being a public firm. However, we also need to take into account motivations specifically related to the choice to go private, that is, motivations that are not derived from the going public literature.

The literature on going private largely focuses on the leveraged buyout as a mechanism to increase the firm value because of improved agency relationships between managers and shareholders, efficiency gains, tax benefits, and wealth transfers from other claimholders. In this section, we provide a summary of the most advocated benefits of leveraged buyouts that will be discussed and extended later.

A leveraged buyout (LBO) is simply a PTP transaction in which the buyer resorts heavily to debt as a primary source of funds. The short-term effects of LBOs on target firms are manifold and can be summarized as follows: (1) the target firm ends up being significantly more indebted than it was before the acquisition; (2) managerial ownership increases significantly; (3) the target firm's shares cease to be publicly traded on the stock market; (4) the ownership structure of the target firm is completely restructured. The long-term effects of LBOs, especially in terms of factors that account for the large premiums over the pre-transaction stock price paid to the target firm's shareholders, were subject to a wide theoretical and empirical debate dating back to the late 1980s.

The explanations typically offered are as follows (Weston et al. 2004): (a) tax benefits; (b) management incentives; (c) wealth transfer effects; (d) information asymmetry and underpricing; (e) efficiency gains. The source of tax benefits is straightforward: higher leverage after the transaction increases the tax savings on interest expense. The increased managerial ownership allows the managers to be strongly rewarded for the performance improvements of the firm. Consequently, they should be highly committed to undertaking profitable projects. Moreover, debt imposes fixed payments that reduce free cash flows available to managers who will therefore be less inclined to waste the firm's resources to the detriment of shareholders (Jensen 1986). Furthermore, since debt increases a firm's earnings volatility and may increase the costs and probability of financial distress, it will put pressure on managers, giving them the incentive to improve the firm's performance and keep bankruptcy risks at bay. Finally, the higher ownership concentration resulting from the buyout induces the largest shareholder (e.g., a private equity firm) to closely monitor the management, leading to lower agency costs.

Some scholars argue that the premiums paid in LBOs represent wealth transfers to shareholders from other stakeholders such as creditors, employees, the government, and so on. For example, the increased debt may worsen the target firm's creditworthiness, leading to a reduction in the price of outstanding bonds. Likewise, the new controlling owner may attempt to renegotiate labor contracts in order to obtain savings on salaries. According to information asymmetry and underpricing theories, managers and buyout investors are likely to be more informed about the value of the firm than dispersed shareholders. The buyout bid is therefore a signal to the market that the firm's future performance will be better than what was previously expected; alternatively, the purchase price paid in LBO was deemed by acquirers to be less than the value of the company and the pre-buyout shareholders are therefore receiving less than adequately informed shareholders would receive. Finally, sources of gains may stem from a more efficient decision-making process under private ownership, that is, actions can be taken more quickly, project implementation can be carried out without the need to prepare detailed reports to be shown to the board of directors and so on.

1.4.11 PTP Transactions When the Ownership Structure Is Highly Concentrated

So far, the characteristics and motivations of PTP transactions apply to any type of firm, but more specifically to firms with dispersed corporate shareholders. In a context characterized by highly concentrated ownership structures, some adaptations both to the structure of the deal and to the motives of the transaction should be made.

Fragmented ownership gives rise to separation between ownership and control (Jensen and Meckling 1976) and the well-known conflict of interests between managers and shareholders (Type I agency costs). In this scenario, the management team (decision agent) does not bear a substantial share of the wealth effects of its decisions. PTP transactions, among other things:

1. allow the firm to improve the realignment of interest between managers and shareholders as a result of the increase in the equity interest held by managers (Kaplan 1989a);
2. reduce the free cash flow problem (Jensen 1986) as a result of the large use of debt and the higher ownership concentration that results from the deal;
3. allow the firm to increase value through tax benefits of debt (Kaplan 1989b).

However, when ownership concentration is high, the firm is generally taken private by the existing controlling shareholders through a tender offer with freeze-out of minority shareholders. Besides, the deal does not necessarily imply a significant increase in debt because the largest shareholders can leverage the company without taking it private (Bajo et al. 2013). As a result, in countries with highly concentrated ownership structures, PTP transactions are differently implemented and, more importantly, the reasons for their execution can be different and cannot be related to the realignment of interest (the control is already in the hands of the largest shareholder), the reduction of the free cash flow problem, and the tax consideration (the use of debt is not usual and the ownership concentration is already high). Therefore, among the many proposed rationales for going private, undervaluation, liquidity considerations, information asymmetry, and control considerations are the ones that are more likely to play a significant role.

Croci and Del Giudice (2014) observe that despite the fact that controlling shareholders have to pay a premium over the pre-transaction stock price to persuade minority shareholders to sell their shares, they may be better informed than minorities on the true value of the company and offer a discounted price compared to what other bidders would have been able to offer. If so, announcement reaction should be lower than that found in comparable delisting. They do not find evidence supporting this assumption. However, Bajo et al. (2013) confirm that controlling shareholders pay a larger premium when they bid for delisting and have to convince institutional shareholders who seem to protect minorities' interests against expropriation risks.

References

Acharya, V. V., & Pedersen, L. H. (2005). Asset pricing with liquidity risk. *Journal of Financial Economics, 77*(2), 375–410.

Acharya, V. V., Franks, J., & Servaes, H. (2007). Private equity: Boom and bust? *Journal of Applied Corporate Finance, 19*(4), 1–10.

Akerlof, G. (1970). The market for lemons. *Quarterly Journal of Economics, 84*(3), 488–500.

Amihud, Y., & Li, K. (2006). The declining information content of dividend announcements and the effects of institutional holdings. *Journal of Financial and Quantitative Analysis, 41*(3), 637–660.

Amihud, Y., & Mendelson, H. (1986). Asset pricing and the bid-ask spread. *Journal of Financial Economics, 17*(2), 223–249.

Amihud, Y., & Mendelson, H. (1988). Liquidity and asset prices: Financial management implications. *Financial Management, 17*(1), 5–15.

Amihud, Y., & Mendelson, H. (1991). Liquidity, asset prices and financial policy. *Financial Analysts Journal, 47*(6), 56–66.

Amihud, Y., & Mendelson, H. (2012). Liquidity, the value of the firm, and corporate finance. *Journal of Applied Corporate Finance, 24*(1), 17–32.

Arbel, A., Carvell, S., & Strebel, P. (1983). Giraffes, institutions and neglected firms. *Financial Analysts Journal, 39*(3), 57–63.

Aslan, H., & Kumar, P. (2011). Lemons or cherries? Growth opportunities and market temptations in going public and private. *Journal of Financial and Quantitative Analysis, 46*(2), 489–526.

Bajo, E., Barbi, M., Bigelli, M., & Hillier, D. (2013). The role of institutional investors in public-to-private transactions. *Journal of Banking & Finance, 37*(11), 4327–4336.

Baker, M., & Stein, J. C. (2004). Market liquidity as a sentiment indicator. *Journal of Financial Markets, 7*(3), 271–299.

Bancel, F., & Mittoo, U. R. (2009). Why do European firms go public? *European Financial Management, 15*(4), 844–884.

Banerjee, S., Gatchev, V. A., & Spindt, P. A. (2007). Stock market liquidity and firm dividend policy. *Journal of Financial and Quantitative Analysis, 42*(2), 369–397.

Barth, M. E., Konchitchki, Y., & Landsman, W. R. (2013). Cost of capital and earnings transparency. *Journal of Accounting and Economics, 55*(2–3), 206–224.

Bebchuk, L., Cohen, A., & Ferrell, A. (2009). What matters in corporate governance? *Review of Financial Studies, 22*(2), 783–827.

Bharath, S. T., & Dittmar, A. K. (2010). Why do firms use private equity to opt out of public markets? *The Review of Financial Studies, 23*(5), 1771–1818.

Bharath, S. T., Pasquariello, P., & Wu, G. (2009). Does asymmetric information drive capital structure decisions? *Review of Financial Studies, 22*(8), 3211–3243.

Bharath, S. T., Dittmar, A. K., & Sivadasan, J. (2014). Do going-private transactions affect plant efficiency and investment? *The Review of Financial Studies, 27*(7), 1929–1976.

Bhide, A. (1990). Reversing corporate diversification. *Journal of Applied Corporate Finance, 3*(2), 70–81.

Bhide, A. (1993). The hidden costs of stock market liquidity. *Journal of Financial Economics, 34*(1), 31–51.

Black, F. (1976). Studies of stock price volatility changes. Proceedings of the 1976 meetings of the American Statistical Association, business and economics statistics section, pp. 177–181.

Bolton, P., & Von Thadden, E. L. (1998). Blocks, liquidity, and corporate control. *The Journal of Finance, 53*(1), 1–25.

Boot, A. W., Gopalan, R., & Thakor, A. V. (2006). The entrepreneur's choice between private and public ownership. *The Journal of Finance, 61*(2), 803–836.

Boot, A. W., Gopalan, R., & Thakor, A. V. (2008). Market liquidity, investor participation, and managerial autonomy: Why do firms go private? *The Journal of Finance, 63*(4), 2013–2059.
Botosan, C. A. (1997). Disclosure level and the cost of equity capital. *The Accounting Review, 72*(3), 323–349.
Brau, J. C., & Fawcett, S. E. (2006). Initial public offerings: An analysis of theory and practice. *The Journal of Finance, 61*(1), 399–436.
Brau, J. C., Francis, B., & Kohers, N. (2003). The choice of IPO versus takeover: Empirical evidence. *Journal of Business, 76*(4), 583–612.
Brav, A., Jiang, W., Partnoy, F., & Thomas, R. (2008). Hedge fund activism, corporate governance, and firm performance. *The Journal of Finance, 63*(4), 1729–1775.
Brennan, M. J., & Subrahmanyam, A. (1995). Investment analysis and price formation in securities markets. *Journal of Financial Economics, 38*(3), 361–381.
Brockman, P., Howe, J. S., & Mortal, S. (2008). Stock market liquidity and the decision to repurchase. *Journal of Corporate Finance, 14*(4), 446–459.
Bushee, B. J., & Leuz, C. (2005). Economic consequences of SEC disclosure regulation: Evidence from the OTC bulletin board. *Journal of Accounting and Economics, 39*(2), 233–264.
Campbell, T. S. (1979). Optimal investment financing decisions and the value of confidentiality. *Journal of Financial and Quantitative Analysis, 14*(5), 913–924.
Chemmanur, T. J., & Fulghieri, P. (1999). A theory of the going-public decision. *The Review of Financial Studies, 12*(2), 249–279.
Coates IV., J. C. (2007). The goals and promise of the Sarbanes-Oxley Act. *Journal of Economic Perspectives, 21*(1), 91–116.
Coffee, J. C. (1991). Liquidity versus control: The institutional investor as corporate monitor. *Columbia Law Review, 91*(6), 1277–1368.
Coller, M., & Yohn, T. L. (1997). Management forecasts and information asymmetry: An examination of bid-ask spreads. *Journal of Accounting Research, 35*(2), 181–191.
Comment, R., & Jarrell, G. A. (1995). Corporate focus and stock returns. *Journal of Financial Economics, 37*(1), 67–87.
Croci, E., & Del Giudice, A. (2014). Delistings, controlling shareholders and firm performance in Europe. *European Financial Management, 20*(2), 374–405.
DeAngelo, H., DeAngelo, L., & Rice, E. M. (1984). Going private: Minority freezeouts and stockholder wealth. *The Journal of Law and Economics, 27*(2), 367–401.
Demirag, I. S. (2015). Short-termism. Wiley Encyclopedia of Management.
Denis, D. J. (1992). Corporate investment decisions and corporate control: Evidence from going-private transactions. *Financial Management, 21*(3), 80–94.
Diamond, D. W., & Verrecchia, R. E. (1991). Disclosure, liquidity, and the cost of capital. *Journal of Finance, 46*(4), 1325–1359.

Draper, P., & Paudyal, K. (2008). Information asymmetry and bidders' gains. *Journal of Business Finance & Accounting, 35*(3–4), 376–405.
Eckbo, B. E., & Masulis, R. W. (1992). Adverse selection and the rights offer paradox. *Journal of Financial Economics, 32*(3), 293–332.
Eckbo, B. E., & Masulis, R. W. (1995). Seasoned equity offerings: A survey, In R. A. Jarrow, V. Maksimovic, & W. T. Ziemba (Ed.), *Handbooks in operations research and management science* (Vol. 9, Chap. 31, pp. 1017–1072). Amsterdam: North-Holland/Elsevier.
Edmans, A., Fang, V. W., & Zur, E. (2013). The effect of liquidity on governance. *The Review of Financial Studies, 26*(6), 1443–1482.
Engel, E., Hayes, R. M., & Wang, X. (2007). The Sarbanes–Oxley Act and firms' going-private decisions. *Journal of Accounting and Economics, 44*(1–2), 116–145.
Fama, E. F., & French, K. R. (1995). Size and book-to-market factors in earnings and returns. *Journal of Finance, 50*(1), 131–155.
Fang, V. W., Noe, T. H., & Tice, S. (2009). Stock market liquidity and firm value. *Journal of Financial Economics, 94*(1), 150–169.
Fazzari, S. M., Hubbard, R. G., Petersen, B. C., Blinder, A. S., & Poterba, J. M. (1988). Financing constraints and corporate investment. *Brookings Papers on Economic Activity, 1988*(1), 141–206.
Fazzari, S. M., Hubbard, R. G., & Petersen, B. C. (2000). Investment-cash flow sensitivities are useful: A comment on Kaplan and Zingales. *The Quarterly Journal of Economics, 115*(2), 695–705.
Fink, J., Fink, K. E., Grullon, G., & Weston, J. P. (2010). What drove the increase in idiosyncratic volatility during the internet boom? *Journal of Financial and Quantitative Analysis, 45*(5), 1253–1278.
Freeman, R. N. (1987). The association between accounting earnings and security returns for large and small firms. *Journal of Accounting and Economics, 9*(2), 195–228.
Gompers, P. A. (1996). Grandstanding in the venture capital industry. *Journal of Financial Economics, 42*(1), 133–156.
Gompers, P. A., Ishii, J., & Metrick, A. (2003). Corporate governance and equity prices. *The Quarterly Journal of Economics, 118*(1), 107–156.
Graham, J. R., Harvey, C. R., & Rajgopal, S. (2005). The economic implications of corporate financial reporting. *Journal of Accounting and Economics, 40*(1–3), 3–73.
Guo, S., Hotchkiss, E. S., & Song, W. (2011). Do buyouts (still) create value? *Journal of Finance, 66*(2), 479–517.
Halling, M., Pagano, M., Randl, O., & Zechner, J. (2008). Where is the market? Evidence from cross-listings in the United States. *The Review of Financial Studies, 21*(2), 725–761.
Hansen, R. S. (1988). The demise of the rights issue. *The Review of Financial Studies, 1*(3), 289–309.

Herman, E. S. (1981). *Corporate control, corporate power*. New York: Cambridge University Press.

Holmstrom, B., & Kaplan, S. N. (2003). The state of US corporate governance: What's right and what's wrong? *Journal of Applied Corporate Finance, 15*(3), 8–20.

Ibbotson, R. G., & Jaffe, J. F. (1975). "Hot issue" markets. *The Journal of Finance, 30*(4), 1027–1042.

Jayaraman, S., & Milbourn, T. T. (2011). The role of stock liquidity in executive compensation. *The Accounting Review, 87*(2), 537–563.

Jensen, M. C. (1986). Agency costs of free cash flow, corporate finance, and takeovers. *The American Economic Review, 76*(2), 323–329.

Jensen, M. C., & Meckling, W. H. (1976). Theory of the firm: Managerial behavior, agency costs and ownership structure. *Journal of Financial Economics, 3*(4), 305–360.

Kamar, E., Karaca-Mandic, P., & Talley, E. (2009). Going-private decisions and the Sarbanes-Oxley Act of 2002: A cross-country analysis. *The Journal of Law, Economics, & Organization, 25*(1), 107–133.

Kaplan, S. N. (1989a). The effects of management buyouts on operating performance and value. *Journal of Financial Economics, 24*(2), 217–254.

Kaplan, S. N. (1989b). Management buyouts: Evidence on taxes as a source of value. *The Journal of Finance, 44*(3), 611–632.

Kaplan, S. N., & Zingales, L. (1997). Do investment-cash flow sensitivities provide useful measures of financing constraints? *The Quarterly Journal of Economics, 112*(1), 169–215.

Kaplan, S. N., & Zingales, L. (2000). Investment-cash flow sensitivities are not valid measures of financing constraints. *The Quarterly Journal of Economics, 115*(2), 707–712.

Kashefi Pour, E., & Lasfer, M. (2013). Why do companies delist voluntarily from the stock market? *Journal of Banking & Finance, 37*(12), 4850–4860.

Kieschnick, R. L. (1989). Management buyouts of public corporations: An analysis of prior characteristics. In Y. Amihud (Ed.), *Leveraged Management Buyouts: Causes and Consequences* (pp. 35–59). Homewood: Dow Jones-Irwin.

Kieschnick, R. L. (1998). Free cash flow and stockholder gains in going private transactions revisited. *Journal of Business Finance & Accounting, 25*(1–2), 187–202.

Kim, W., & Weisbach, M. S. (2008). Motivations for public equity offers: An international perspective. *Journal of Financial Economics, 87*(2), 281–307.

Kothare, M. (1997). The effects of equity issues on ownership structure and stock liquidity: A comparison of rights and public offerings. *Journal of Financial Economics, 43*(1), 131–148.

Lehn, K., & Poulsen, A. (1989). Free cash flow and stockholder gains in going private transactions. *The Journal of Finance, 44*(3), 771–787.

Leland, H. E., & Pyle, D. H. (1977). Informational asymmetries, financial structure, and financial intermediation. *The Journal of Finance, 32*(2), 371–387.

Lerner, J. (1994). Venture capitalists and the decision to go public. *Journal of Financial Economics, 35*(3), 293–316.
Leuz, C. (2007). Was the Sarbanes–Oxley Act of 2002 really this costly? A discussion of evidence from event returns and going-private decisions. *Journal of Accounting and Economics, 44*(1–2), 146–165.
Leuz, C., Nanda, D., & Wysocki, P. D. (2003). Earnings management and investor protection: An international comparison. *Journal of Financial Economics, 69*(3), 505–527.
Loughran, T., Ritter, J. R., & Rydqvist, K. (1994). Initial public offerings: International insights. *Pacific-Basin Finance Journal, 2*(2–3), 165–199.
Lowenstein, L. (1985). Management buyouts. *Columbia Law Review, 85*(4), 730–784.
Lowry, M. (2003). Why does IPO volume fluctuate so much? *Journal of Financial Economics, 67*(1), 3–40.
Lucas, D. J., & McDonald, R. L. (1990). Equity issues and stock price dynamics. *The Journal of Finance, 45*(4), 1019–1043.
Marosi, A., & Massoud, N. (2007). Why do firms go dark? *Journal of Financial and Quantitative Analysis, 42*(2), 421–442.
Masulis, R. W., & Thomas, R. S. (2009). Does private equity create wealth? The effects of private equity and derivatives on corporate governance. *The University of Chicago Law Review, 76*(1), 219–259.
Maug, E. (1998). Large shareholders as monitors: Is there a trade-off between liquidity and control? *The Journal of Finance, 53*(1), 65–98.
Maupin, R. J., Bidwell, C. M., & Ortegren, A. K. (1984). An empirical investigation of the characteristics of publicly-quoted corporations which change to closely-held ownership through management buyouts. *Journal of Business Finance & Accounting, 11*(4), 435–450.
Mehran, H., & Peristiani, S. (2010). Financial visibility and the decision to go private. *The Review of Financial Studies, 23*(2), 519–547.
Mello, A. S., & Parsons, J. E. (1998). Going public and the ownership structure of the firm. *Journal of Financial Economics, 49*(1), 79–109.
Merton, R. C. (1987). A simple model of capital market equilibrium with incomplete information. *The Journal of Finance, 42*(3), 483–510.
Merton, R. C. (1995). Financial innovation and the management and regulation of financial institutions. *Journal of Banking & Finance, 19*(3–4), 461–481.
Metrick, A., & Yasuda, A. (2010). The economics of private equity funds. *The Review of Financial Studies, 23*(6), 2303–2341.
Miller, M. H., & Modigliani, F. (1961). Dividend policy, growth, and the valuation of shares. *Journal of Business, 34*(4), 411–433.
Mitchell, M. L., & Mulherin, J. H. (1996). The impact of industry shocks on takeover and restructuring activity. *Journal of Financial Economics, 41*(2), 193–229.

Muscarella, C. J., & Vetsuypens, M. R. (1990). Efficiency and organizational structure: A study of reverse LBOs. *The Journal of Finance, 45*(5), 1389–1413.
Myers, S. C. (1977). Determinants of corporate borrowing. *Journal of Financial Economics, 5*(2), 147–175.
Myhal, P. J. (1990). Some observations on the usual anti-dilution provisions. *Canadian Business Law Journal, 17*(2), 283–302.
Opler, T., & Titman, S. (1993). The determinants of leveraged buyout activity: Free cash flow vs. financial distress costs. *The Journal of Finance, 48*(5), 1985–1999.
Pagano, M., & Röell, A. (1998). The choice of stock ownership structure: Agency costs, monitoring, and the decision to go public. *The Quarterly Journal of Economics, 113*(1), 187–225.
Pagano, M., Panetta, F., & Zingales, L. (1998). Why do companies go public? An empirical analysis. *The Journal of Finance, 53*(1), 27–64.
Pástor, Ľ., & Stambaugh, R. F. (2003). Liquidity risk and expected stock returns. *Journal of Political Economy, 111*(3), 642–685.
Perotti, E. C., & Van Oijen, P. (2001). Privatization, political risk and stock market development in emerging economies. *Journal of International Money and Finance, 20*(1), 43–69.
Pettit, R. R., & Singer, R. F. (1985). Small business finance: A research agenda. *Financial Management, 14*(3), 47–60.
Ritter, J. R. (1984). The "hot issue" market of 1980. *Journal of Business, 57*(2), 215–240.
Ritter, J. R., & Welch, I. (2002). A review of IPO activity, pricing, and allocations. *The Journal of Finance, 57*(4), 1795–1828.
Roulstone, D. T. (2003). Analyst following and market liquidity. *Contemporary Accounting Research, 20*(3), 552–578.
Rydqvist, K., & Högholm, K. (1995). Going public in the 1980s: Evidence from Sweden. *European Financial Management, 1*(3), 287–315.
Servaes, H. (1994). Do takeover targets overinvest? *The Review of Financial Studies, 7*(2), 253–277.
Shah, S., & Thakor, A. V. (1988). Private versus public ownership: Investment, ownership distribution, and optimality. *The Journal of Finance, 43*(1), 41–59.
Shleifer, A., & Vishny, R. W. (1988). Management's buyouts as a response to market pressure. In A. Auerbach (Ed.), *Mergers and acquisitions* (pp. 87–103). Chicago: The University of Chicago Press.
Shleifer, A., & Vishny, R. W. (1997). A survey of corporate governance. *The Journal of Finance, 52*(2), 737–783.
Singh, A. K. (1997). Layoffs and underwritten rights offers. *Journal of Financial Economics, 43*(1), 105–130.

Slovin, M. B., Sushka, M. E., & Lai, K. W. (2000). Alternative flotation methods, adverse selection, and ownership structure: Evidence from seasoned equity issuance in the UK. *Journal of Financial Economics, 57*(2), 157–190.
Smith Jr., C. W. (1977). Alternative methods for raising capital: Rights versus underwritten offerings. *Journal of Financial Economics, 5*(3), 273–307.
Smith, A. J. (1990). Corporate ownership structure and performance: The case of management buyouts. *Journal of Financial Economics, 27*(1), 143–164.
Stein, J. C. (1989). Efficient capital markets, inefficient firms: A model of myopic corporate behavior. *The Quarterly Journal of Economics, 104*(4), 655–669.
Stoughton, N. M., & Zechner, J. (1998). IPO-mechanisms, monitoring and ownership structure. *Journal of Financial Economics, 49*(1), 45–77.
Strömberg, P. (2007). *The new demography of private equity*. Swedish Institute for Financial Research, Stockholm School of Economics, CEPR and NBER, working paper.
Subrahmanyam, A., & Titman, S. (1999). The going-public decision and the development of financial markets. *The Journal of Finance, 54*(3), 1045–1082.
Verrecchia, R. E. (1983). Discretionary disclosure. *Journal of Accounting and Economics, 5*, 179–194.
Verrecchia, R. E. (1990). Information quality and discretionary disclosure. *Journal of Accounting and Economics, 12*(4), 365–380.
Weston, J. F., Mitchell, M. L., & Mulherin, J. H. (2004). *Takeovers, restructuring, and corporate governance* (4th ed.). Upper Saddle River: Pearson-Prentice Hall.
Yosha, O. (1995). Information disclosure costs and the choice of financing source. *Journal of Financial Intermediation, 4*(1), 3–20.
Zingales, L. (1994). The value of the voting right: A study of the Milan stock exchange experience. *The Review of Financial Studies, 7*(1), 125–148.
Zingales, L. (1995). Insider ownership and the decision to go public. *The Review of Economic Studies, 62*(3), 425–448.
Zingales, L. (2007). Is the US capital market losing its competitive edge? European Corporate Governance Institute. Finance Working Paper n. 192.

CHAPTER 2

Leveraged Buyouts, Going Dark and the Change of the Trading Venue

Ottorino Morresi

2.1 Leveraged Buyouts: Introduction

Michael Jensen, in one of his most cited essays (Jensen 1989), casted doubt on the role of the public corporation as the main engine of the US economic development. He claimed that new organizations were emerging in its place that were characterized by the following elements: (1) no public shareholders; (2) no listed and traded shares; (3) use of public and private debt instead of public equity as their major source of capital; (4) large institutions and entrepreneurs, rather than households, as the primary shareholders that appoint agents to manage and monitor on their behalf and bind those agents with large equity interests and contracts governing the distribution of cash.

The most evident manifestation of this organizational change can be found in the huge growth of deals such as takeovers, corporate breakups, divisional spin-offs, leveraged buyouts, and PTP transactions in general that dominated the scene in the 1980s. According to Jensen (1989), these new organizational forms were arising in response to the central weakness of the public corporation—the conflict between managers and shareholders over the control and use of corporate resources—that resulted in enormous waste and mismanagement especially from the mid-1960s to the early 1970s.

B. Fidanza et al., *The Decision to Delist from the Stock Market*,
https://doi.org/10.1007/978-3-319-95049-5_2

That period of misconduct triggered the organizational transformation of the 1980s. Of course, this does not mean that the public corporation will be totally replaced by this new organizational form; it continues to be a viable option in sectors such as biotechnology, pharmaceuticals, electronics, and so on, characterized by a surplus of profitable investment opportunities. Firms in these sectors are less likely to waste resources systematically and have to turn regularly to the capital markets to raise funds required to supplement the insufficient internally generated cash flows. In contrast, the public corporation is not suitable in industries characterized by slow long-term growth and with internally generated funds exceeding the amount of profitable projects. In these cash-rich, low-growth sectors, the pressure on management to waste cash flows through investments in unsound projects can be very high. It is in precisely these sectors that the publicly held corporation has declined most rapidly.

We can argue that these new organizations are short on the beneficial characteristics that are supposed to be unique to the public corporation, that is, its capacity to spread financial risk over the diversified portfolios of millions of individuals and institutions, its capacity to allow investors to customize risk to their unique circumstances and predilections, and its capacity to allow risk to be borne by investors best able to bear it, without requiring them to manage the corporations they own.

Indeed, the power of this new organizational form is that it allows the firm to avoid most of the losses created by the conflict between managers and shareholders, without giving up the functions of risk diversification and liquidity which was once performed exclusively by the public equity market. In what follows, we will discuss origin, trends, structure, benefits, and costs of the most widespread of these organizational forms, the leveraged buyout.

2.2 Origin, Trends, and Characteristics

First of all, let's clarify once again that there is much overlap in LBOs and going private transactions. LBO is more precisely a financing technique used by a variety of entities such as management, other corporations, private equity firms, investment coalitions, and so on, to purchase a company by relying heavily on debt. This technique is frequently employed by these entities to take a public firm private. This explains why we refer to LBO as a PTP transaction. However, PTP transactions can also be carried out without resorting to debt and not all LBOs are PTP transactions.

Although LBO activity is deemed to have its origins in the 1980s, it has a longer history dating back to the 1970s when the stock market turned down in 1973–1974 and the price of some low-quality firms fell dramatically. During that period, cheap market valuations induced the managers of some of the firms that went public in the 1960s to take their companies private (Lowenstein 1985). In addition, many conglomerates that were built up in the 1960s through large-scale acquisitions began to become partially disassembled through selloffs. Part of this process of deconglomeration took place through the sale of divisions of conglomerates through LBOs.

This process was ongoing throughout the 1980s (the first wave of LBOs) after which it faced a period of correction in the early 1990s. After 1992 until 2000, there was a second wave of LBOs that stopped in 2001 when the stock market fell in 2001–2002. The third wave started in 2003 and ended in 2007 with the collapse of the subprime mortgage market that caused a sharp tightening of credit conditions, a widening of credit spreads, a stock market crash, and a diffused liquidity crisis that interrupted the relaxed and favorable market conditions that fueled these transactions in the previous years. Each wave has its own distinctive characteristics in terms of debt raised, financial instruments used to finance the transaction, premium paid, type of investors involved in the deal, economic conditions during which the wave occurred, and so on.

In the first wave of LBOs, debt financing normally represented far more than 50% of the purchase price. Debt was secured by the assets of the acquired firm or based on the expected future cash flows. It was scheduled to be paid off either by selling the target firm's assets or by using the future cash flows generated by the operations. After completing the buyout, the target firm became a privately held corporation. The acquired firm was expected to go public again after a period of three to five years at a gain. The 1980s LBO wave was fueled by the following main factors (Morresi and Pezzi 2014).

First, was the need to respond to the failure of internal governance mechanisms of US corporations. Ever since the 1930s, management incentives had become weaker as corporations had become larger, management ownership had shrunk, and shareholders had become more dispersed. Boards that were supposed to be the guardians of shareholder rights mostly sided with management and were ineffective in performing their duties. Among the biggest drawbacks of corporations, there was the propensity to subsidize poorly performing divisions by draining cash from successful ones, instead of returning cash flows to investors. This misconduct was particularly pronounced in the 1970s, triggered by the process of conglomeration dating back to the 1960s. In this context, LBOs came into play as a successful governance mechanism aimed at minimizing the waste of resources that characterized the 1960s and the 1970s (Jensen 1989).

A related story on LBO-induced better governance mechanisms is that the first LBO wave was to a large extent in response to the disappointment with conglomerates (Shleifer and Vishny 1991). Corporate diversification was increasingly demonstrated to be a value destroying strategy (e.g., Berger and Ofek 1995; Lang and Stulz 1994; Rajan et al. 2000). This made many conglomerates assembled in the 1960s targets of hostile takeovers as a result of their depressed stock market valuations compared with those of single-segment firms (the so-called diversification discount[1]).

Second, was a period of sustained economic growth between 1983 and 1990. The US GDP growth rate was uninterruptedly positive from 1983 to 1990, peaking at 7% in 1984. Total M&A transactions reached a peak in 1986 in terms of the number of transactions whereas LBOs peaked in 1988.

Third, was persistent (unexpected) inflation. Since the late 1960s, double-digit or close to that level inflation showed up in a large portion of the period from the late 1960s to the 1980s. Inflation promoted LBOs in different ways. First, it resulted in a sharp decline of the q-ratio, that is, the ratio of the market value of a firm to the replacement cost of its assets. A q-ratio less than 1 means that it is cheaper to buy capacity in the financial markets than in the real asset markets. The q-ratio moved from a peak of 1.30 in 1965 to a low of 0.52 in 1981. It began to rise in 1982 as a result of the stock market growth. The relatively cheap market valuations stimulated all types of acquisitions, including LBOs.

Second, inflation spurred the use of debt financing because of the ability to realize consistent tax savings. In fact, while most coupon payments of outstanding bonds were not inflation-indexed due to the unexpected period of high inflation, real debt obligations declined with rising price levels. This meant that the leverage ratio in real terms decreased severely during that period, thereby stimulating leveraged recapitalizations and other leverage-increasing deals.

Third, on the asset side, inflation caused free cash flows to increase. This, coupled with fixed interest payments on existing debt, exacerbated agency costs of free cash flow and made those firms that delayed increasing their debt ratio attractive targets to outside investors able and willing to carry out the restructuring. The increased inclination toward restructuring strategies, in turn, stimulated new forms of debt financing such as junk

[1] Recent studies cast doubt on the existence of the diversification discount (e.g., Campa and Kedia 2002; Villalonga 2004a, b).

bonds. The latter were also promoted by the increasingly aggressive presence of investment bankers that developed new and more sophisticated financial instruments to help finance the deals[2] and by the succession of laws that contributed to deregulating financial institutions.

Fourth, was the role of deregulation. In the 1980s some industries such as air transport, broadcasting, entertainment, natural gas, and trucking underwent significant federal deregulation that radically changed the forces of competition, therefore creating room for value gains by recombining the businesses.

Fifth, was legislative changes. New tax laws stimulated restructuring and takeover activity. In particular, the Economic Recovery Tax Act (ERTA) of 1981 allowed old assets to be stepped up on purchase. These newly established high values could then be depreciated on an accelerated basis. In a period of high inflation, the nominal value of corporate assets was increased above their historical cost, enabling a large step-up in basis[3]. Also under the General Utilities doctrine which was repealed by the Tax Reform Act of 1986, the sale of assets in the liquidation process was not subject to capital gain taxes at the corporate level. The new fiscal treatment of employee stock option plans (ESOPs) promoted management buyouts (MBOs). According to the new regulation, the firm was able to treat as a deductible expense for tax purposes contributions to the ESOP that were sufficient to cover the interest and the principal payments on the loan. It increased the ability of ESOPs to borrow from a bank to invest the funds in the firm's share. Moreover, a further tax law change enacted in 1984 allowed banks to deduct half of their interest income on loans to ESOPs. This allowed the banks to make loans to ESOPs on relatively better terms. This clause was repealed in 1996.

The sixth and final factor was, the new antitrust climate of the 1980s. New appointees to the Federal Trade Commission and the Department of Justice claimed that the stringent prohibitions against vertical and

[2] For example, the failed Drexel Burnham Lambert was the pioneer investment bank that developed the junk bond market.

[3] The effects of the change in the tax regime were controversial. Scholes and Wolfson (1990) show that the passage of ERTA in 1981 stimulated reorganization activities, including LBOs. However, Schipper and Smith (1991) find that, although depreciation tax deductions arising from ERTA were generally positive for the firms that announced asset write-ups, they were not a significant source of gains in a number of management buyouts during the period 1982–1986. In the same vein as Schipper and Smith (1991), Kaplan (1989b) finds that while asset step-up elections had a positive value when made, they were not the driving force behind management buyouts.

horizontal mergers would no longer be supported. The policy change in the antitrust regulatory environment was explained by three main interpretations. First, the new administration had different political views. Second, a decade of empirical researches carried out by the academic community provided support for a dynamic competition view of the interactions among large firms. Third, the most relevant US industries became subject to intense competition from foreign firms. Consequently, increased competitive pressures stimulated restructuring strategies and the acknowledgment of these new pressures laid the foundations for a change in public opinion and the regulatory policy regarding M&As.

Why did the first LBO wave terminate? A number of different factors came into play. First of all, Federal Reserve responded to the lengthy peacetime expansion of the 1980s by raising interest rates from 1986 to 1989. This weakened but did not stop growth, but some combination of the subsequent 1990 oil price shock, the debt accumulation of the 1980s, and growing consumer pessimism combined with the weakened economy to produce a brief recession in the early 1990s (from July 1990 to March 1991). The stock market anticipated this period of recession and experienced a small drop in 1990.

Second, LBOs made in the second half of the 1980s were qualitatively far poorer than those made in the first half. Quality deterioration was due to the fact that an economy segment such as that of LBOs characterized by high returns attracts a large amount of financial resources: new firms and funds specialized in LBOs were formed, and banks and other financial institutions increasingly participated, also persuaded by the rich fees. Consequently, the volume of resources conveyed to the LBO segment began to exceed the number of available good deals. This gave rise to the well-known Winner's Curse phenomenon according to which LBOs in the second half of the 1980s were completed at multiples that were far higher than those of the earlier transactions. In other words, the increased competition driven by the growth in the number of LBO investors as well as the excess of resources compared with the availability of good prospects caused the winning bidders to pay too much.

Third, public high-yield debt substituted for private subordinated debt and strip financing in which subordinated debt holders also received equity stakes. This raised the cost of reorganizing companies that encountered financial difficulties. Fourth, commercial banks began to reduce their exposure. In particular, they sought to reduce their commitments, shorten debt maturities, and required accelerated repayments of the principal amount. This led to a severe reduction of debt service coverage ratios that, in some cases, forced the firm to sell assets or cut costs immediately in order to pay the first interest installment.

Adverse economic contingencies went together with a less favorable legislative environment. In 1989, Congress passed the Financial Institutions Reform, Recovery and Enforcement Act (FIRREA) which dramatically changed the savings and loan (S&L) industry and its federal regulation. One of its major effects was to push huge amounts of junk debt from S&L portfolios onto the marketplace, severely depressing the market of high-yield bonds that was devastated by the bankruptcy of some of the largest junk bond issuers and buyers such as LTV Corporation, Integrated Resources, Drexel Burnham Lambert, during the second half of the 1980s. Moreover, banking authorities induced banks to reduce their exposure to highly leveraged transactions. All of this resulted in a significant correction in the LBO market characterized by lower transaction prices, larger equity commitments, lower debt ratios, and lower upfront fees.

The second wave of LBOs (1992–2000) was partially fueled by the same factors that triggered the first one but with some relevant differences. First, as for the first wave, since 1992, the US economy had been experiencing a period of sustained growth: share prices reached new highs, with a double-digit stock market growth in almost all the years of the period and the size of the junk bond market regained record levels. However, during the second wave, the use of junk bonds as a means to finance large acquisitions no longer plays the same role as in the first wave, marking the decline of this instrument as the most used source of funds in LBOs. Indeed, the second wave of LBOs was also characterized by smaller and more numerous transactions than those in the 1980s: mega-LBOs such as the $25 billion acquisition of RJR Nabisco by KKR in 1988 disappeared almost completely in the 1990s.

Second, the financial structure of the typical LBO changed: first, the deals were completed at multiples that were far lower than those in the 1980s (e.g., the 1980s typical LBO was completed at a price-to-EBITDA ratio of 7–8, with peaks of 10; in the 1990s, the ratio dropped to 5–6); second, the percentage of equity in the initial capital structure moved from 5%–10% in the 1980s to 20%–30% in the LBOs of the 1990s. The interest coverage ratio increased as well: the EBITDA to interest ratio stabilized at 2, in contrast to the 1980s deals in which the firm was required to sell assets and immediately improve efficiency and profitability to meet interest payments and other financial outlays in the first year of the LBO.

Third, financial intermediaries were also restructured: Drexel Burnham Lambert and other aggressive firms that almost exclusively specialized in LBOs were increasingly replaced by other, more conservative institutional capital suppliers such as private equity firms willing to use less debt and more of their own resources that could also come from other institutional investors such as pension funds, commercial banks, insurance companies, and so on. This sustained the growth of LBOs sponsored by private equity (PE) funds.

Fourth, unlike the LBOs in the 1980s, almost exclusively directed toward mature, cash-generating, and slow-growing firms, the second wave of LBOs also involved high-growth, technology-driven industries. The change of the characteristics of the target firms was also a result of the increased proportion of equity in the financial structure that also made the deals feasible for firms with greater intangible assets and a level of investment opportunities that was disproportionately higher than internally generated funds.

After the correction period of 2001–2002 due to adverse economic and market conditions, the LBOs resumed growth and reached all-time levels. According to Strömberg (2007), more than 40% of LBOs that occurred during the period 1970–2007 have taken place since 2004, that is, during the third wave. Most of these deals, 80%, were private equity deals where a financial sponsor or LBO fund backs the deal and provides most of the equity capital. The motivation behind LBOs no longer appears to be primarily about solving governance problems in US publicly traded firms. Rather, LBO transactions occur worldwide in a variety of industries and target both private and public companies. Moreover, in the third wave, secondary buyouts, where one LBO sponsor exits its investment by selling the firm to a new LBO fund sponsor, became increasingly popular, implying that this organizational form was taking a more permanent form.

A further interesting characteristic of the third wave is its globalization: the number and value of European LBOs increased dramatically after 1996 (Wright et al. 2006) and since 2000 LBOs in Europe have been exceeding by far those completed in the US. In the third wave, some mega-LBOs reappeared and, surprisingly, targeted European firms such as TDC A/S, Wind Telecomunicazioni spa, VNU NV, and so on, rather than US firms that were less involved in large LBOs in the 2000s. However, despite these mega-deals, the average value of European LBOs was below that of the US, showing that more LBOs were completed in Europe but, on average, they were somewhat smaller than LBOs that took place in the US. LBO transactions outside of North America and Western Europe were relatively few and only accounted for approximately 13% of global LBO transactions in number and 7% in value over the period 2001–2007 (Strömberg 2007). This implies that LBO business is largely centered in the US and Europe, although the LBO deal volume in Asia has increased significantly from its level in the 1990s.

The second and third wave therefore show that the original motivations and characteristics of LBOs no longer appear to be representative of the LBO market in the 1990s and 2000s (Holmstrom and Kaplan 2001). Why do LBOs in the 1990s and 2000s look so different compared with those of the first wave? Holmstrom and Kaplan (2001) claim that in the 1990s, corporations began to pursue shareholder-friendly policies, that is, they began to emulate many of the beneficial attributes of LBO structures such as a greater use of incentive-based compensation; a better focus on the aim to make projects that earn a return on capital higher than the cost of capital by developing value-based performance measures such as Economic Value Added (EVA), Total Business Return (TBR), and so on which were used to monitor and reward managers (Venanzi 2012); improved monitoring by shareholders on management arising from the significant growth of institutional investors in the firms' ownership structure. This also led to an increase in shareholder activism; the increased ability of the boards to successfully carry out their tasks in the best interest of shareholders as a result of their smaller size; the higher fraction of the equity-based pay in the directors' compensation packages; the better quality of the CEO turnover process characterized by a marked increase of forced resignations and a greater incidence of CEO outside successions.

In sum, hostile, highly leveraged takeovers, intended to restore superior governance mechanisms, were not necessary anymore[4]. These types of LBOs were substituted with friendly, private-equity-financed transactions whose motives go well beyond the scope of improving the corporate governance of target firms.

[4] The position of Holmstrom and Kaplan (2001) was not shared by many scholars, in particular by Bebchuk and Fried (2004) who asserted that senior management continues to dominate the corporate boards of most publicly held firms in the US and elsewhere. There is substantial evidence of this dominance, including excess CEO compensation, low sensitivity between CEO pay and performance, low sensitivity between CEO performance and turnover, low debt levels leading to unnecessarily large tax payments, minimal restrictions on senior managers' sales or hedging of firm equity, and general support by boards for strong takeover defenses.

The main distinguishing characteristics of the last wave pertain to:

1. The target industry: Although mature industries such as chemicals, machinery, and retailing still provide popular buyout targets, the fraction of LBOs undertaken in high-growth, high-tech sectors such as computers and biotech, has been growing significantly in the last wave. The drop in activity is particularly pronounced in the retail sector which accounted for almost 14% of the number of transactions in the 1970s and 1980s, compared to less than 6% of transactions in the 2000s (Strömberg 2007). One potential explanation is that the changing industry mix of LBOs simply reflects a change in the industry composition in the economy as a whole. Alternatively, it may be the case that private equity firms are deliberately broadening their industry scope beyond the mature, high cash flow, high debt capacity type of industries that they initially targeted;
2. The holding period: LBO organizational form seems more long-term than temporary. The median firm undergoing the original LBO in the 1980s exited LBO status after 6–7 years whereas the median LBO firm in the period 1995–1999 was exited in about 9 years (Kaplan 1991; Strömberg 2007). This is consistent with the expectations of Jensen (1989) who predicted that leveraged buyouts would eventually become a dominant organizational form, implying that LBO ownership is a long-term optimal structure, but it is in contrast to Rappaport (1990) who argued that LBOs were a transitory organizational form which allowed inefficient, badly performing firms with inferior corporate governance to enter a quick but intense period of corporate and governance restructuring in order to return to public ownership in a few years. The growth of secondary buyouts as an exit route may help explain the extended holding period;
3. Globalization: The LBO form has become a global phenomenon, first spreading to Europe and then to other parts of the world such as Asia and Australia;
4. Aggressive use of debt: LBOs in the 1990s and 2000s were executed by using far lower debt levels and resorting to junk bonds to a limited extent;
5. Unprecedented growth of private equity industry: In the 1990s and 2000s the growth of private equity industry was probably the most

> important factor that allowed the LBO market to regain record levels. Recent estimates (e.g., Acharya et al. 2007) show that in 2005–2006, the private-equity/LBO market had reached 5% of the capitalization of the US stock market, or about 1.4% of global GDP. The rapid growth in this market arose from favorable credit market conditions, a huge increase in the size of PE funds' resources, and the increased importance of hedge funds. The tumultuous development of PE funds made it possible to collect extraordinary amounts of resources to be channeled into the LBO business by soliciting investments from various large investors such as pension funds, banks, insurance companies, wealthy individuals, and so on[5].

The third wave also came to an end. In late 2007, private-equity-financed deals dropped off sharply. Increasing competition among bidders had driven deal prices higher, while accommodating credit markets permitted the average multiple of debt to cash flow to rise to historically high levels. High prices and greater debt loads increased default risks for LBO targets. Things broke up when the credit market for private equity leveraged financing seized up around the same time as the subprime mortgage market collapsed.

Not only did this stop new financing from being raised for new private-equity deals, but it also left huge inventories of debt instruments on the books of major banks from older deals that they had already completed, as

[5] Metrick and Yasuda (2010) document that virtually all PE funds are set up as private limited partnerships with a ten-year term in which outside investors (e.g., banks, pension funds, insurance companies, etc.) act as passive limited partners and the PE firm is the controlling general partner. Limited partners have limited or no withdrawal rights prior to the expiration of the ten-year term. They are also potentially subject to additional capital calls by the PE general partner. Most PE firms use similar financing techniques in acquiring portfolio companies. The typical LBO is structured as a purchase of all of the publicly held stocks of a corporation by a privately held acquisition vehicle. A PE buyout firm generally controls this entity, with other types of buyers being much less common. The PE firm sponsoring the transaction will obtain its capital from the equity contributions of its buyout fund which, in turn, raises its capital from outside investors, and of the managers of the target firm plus the cash proceeds from privately placed loans secured by target firm assets and expected cash flows. As part of the acquisition, managers of the target firm obtain a significant equity interest in the firm. Normally, top managers in private-equity-owned firms have equity interests that are ten to twenty times larger than those held by their public company counterparts. After the acquisition, the general partners in the PE fund are actively involved in the strategic direction of the portfolio company.

well as a large pipeline of commitments to finance existing deals. A related problem was the decline in the quality of many of the securities being used to finance these transactions. Financial institutions originating the bank loans that were financing the vast upsurge in private-equity deals were not retaining these loans on their own books, but were rather syndicating them and selling them into the secondary market. Since the originating banks were realizing large fees upfront and then reselling these securities to third parties, the originating banks' incentives to carefully assess the risks of each loan, screen out weak applicants, and monitor their ongoing health were significantly weakened. This created incentives for excessive risk taking in the LBO market. Compounding this problem, many of these deals used "covenant-lite" debt, where, due to highly competitive credit market conditions, LBO lenders agreed to accept weaker contractual protections that reduced lenders' abilities to constrain or discourage opportunistic managerial conduct in these newly privatized firms.

2.3 The Costs and Benefits of LBOs

One of the most widely investigated research questions regarding LBOs, dating back to the late 1980s, is why the bidder is willing to pay such a large premium, often 40% or more, over the price at which shares are traded one to two months before the announcement of the buyout to the target firm's shareholders. One could argue that the sources of gains in LBOs are the same as any other merger or acquisition such as economies of scale and scope, diversification, risk reduction, lower borrowing costs, improved debt capacity, industry consolidation, vertical integration, efficiency gains, monopoly gains, new managerial skills, and so on (Ahern and Weston 2007). The issue is that many of these reasons may not be relevant to LBOs because they do not share some of the distinctive characteristics of "traditional" M&As. First, at least initially, LBO targets remain independent and cannot be combined with another entity to realize synergies. Second, the acquiring firm is often a PE firm whose portfolio companies are managed by different management teams, without any possibility of integration with the participating firms. Consequently, LBOs should have distinctive sources of gains that may account for the high premium paid to the target firm's shareholders.

2.3.1 Improved Agency Relationships

According to Masulis and Thomas (2009), the most commonly cited argument for LBOs creating value is that these transactions enhance corporate governance, therefore lead to agency-cost reductions. The literature has proposed several theories that may account for the improved corporate governance of LBO structures. First, in the Jensen (1986) control hypothesis, LBOs reduce the agency costs of equity by cutting down on managers' discretion to misallocate cash into empire building and excessive perquisites. Empire building and empire preservation in the face of poor performance are directly contrary to the shareholders' interest. Unlike dividends, stock repurchases, and other cash-distributing instruments which can be controlled by managers with greater discretion, adding debt to a company's capital structure is a more credible commitment by management to pay out future cash flows, rather than investing them in negative NPV projects. Thus, executives' single-minded concern for generating cash flow to pay down a company's high debt from an LBO shifts the focus of management from expanding the business in slow-growth areas to growing a company's equity value as rapidly as possible, even if it involves reducing sales and shedding assets that have greater value outside the company. By issuing debt in exchange for equity, managers bond themselves to pay out future cash flows and not to retain or reinvest them in unprofitable ventures.

A related version of the control hypothesis is that debt not only keeps free cash flows away from managerial control, but also increases the bankruptcy risk. This may result in replacement of the current managers so that debt suppliers are given the right to come into possession of a firm's assets if a failure to meet debt service payments occurs. Consequently, managers are induced to try and make the firm as efficient as possible and avoid this risk. A related idea is that leverage may tie managers' hands and commit them to pursue strategies with greater vigor than they would without the threat of financial distress (Perotti and Spier 1993). Finally, when the firm is highly leveraged, creditors themselves will closely monitor the actions of managers, providing an additional layer of management oversight (Harris and Raviv 1990).

Second, LBOs assure a strong realignment of managerial incentives by increasing ownership concentration in the hands of managers (Jensen and Meckling 1976; Jensen 1986). LBO transactions give managers substantial equity ownership positions, resulting in strong financial incentives to work hard and ensure their companies perform well. Kaplan (1989a) estimated that the median pre-buyout ownership of the CEO and all managers were 1.40% and 5.88% respectively. After the transaction, the median ownership stake grew to 6.40% and 22.63%, respectively. Top managers also frequently receive large stock and cash bonuses when they perform well and that may further increase managerial ownership.

A related interpretation of LBO-induced better management incentives is that, according to Easterbrook and Fischel (1982), some profitable investment proposals call for a disproportionate effort on the part of manager-owners. These proposals, which carry provisions for correspondingly disproportionate sharing of investment outcome among manager-owners and outside shareholders, can be seen as being overly generous to managers and can lead to expensive legal contests between insider-managers and outside shareholders. LBO can generate productive gains to the extent that private ownership facilitates compensation arrangements that induce manager-owners to undertake more of these profitable projects.

A third potential cause for reduced agency costs is the enhanced management incentives caused by an intensified sensitivity of stock prices to firm performance. The rise in leverage, which occurs at the time of the LBO, raises the elasticity of stock price revisions to firm value changes (e.g., Galai and Masulis 1976). Thus, managers holding large equity positions achieve much greater wealth gains from improved firm profitability. This intensifies manager incentives both to reduce costs and to increase revenues in order to raise firm value.

Fourth, agency-cost reductions in LBO transactions arise from improved monitoring of the management by the board as a result of much stronger financial incentives for directors and better internal reporting. Basically, the LBO creates a shareholder with a large block of shares, or blockholder, whose representatives are placed on the board and given majority control, whereas management has much more limited board representation. This increased concentration of ownership and control rights eliminates the free rider problem of monitoring management that is endemic to most public corporations. Private-equity board members also have significant financial skills and experience from their prior LBO investments whereas public directors generally do not, and they also have better information to work with. All of these factors together result in better monitoring.

Fifth, Kaplan and Stromberg (2009) emphasize that LBOs can be viewed as an opportunity to replace ineffective senior managers with highly talented executives. The ability of a privately held firm to quickly replace management, which can be entrenched in a publicly held firm, and locate and recruit highly talented executives to the firm by offering them much higher, performance-sensitive compensation is another important element of the LBO process. For example, Acharya et al. (2009) show that one-third of CEOs are replaced within the first 100 days of an LBO and two-thirds are gone within 4 years.

Finally, LBOs may reduce agency costs by eliminating asymmetric information problems between managers and outside investors that may induce managers to undertake less profitable projects. When managerial performance is difficult to evaluate for outside shareholders, incumbent management can be mistakenly replaced. This means that managers could be forced to carry out less profitable projects but with payoffs that are more easily observable by outsiders, in order to defend their position against potential proxy contestants and outside shareholders. By taking the firm private, manager-owners are protected from the actions of less informed outside shareholders who insist on taking investment projects which, although less profitable than other opportunities, have payoffs that are more easily observable by outsiders. Similarly, taking the firm private provides managers with greater influence over the compensation of the board of directors and this reduces the likelihood that difficult-to-evaluate proposals will be resisted or vetoed by relatively uninformed outside directors (DeAngelo and DeAngelo 1985; Travlos and Cornett 1993).

2.3.2 *Tax Benefits*

Another very popular source of gains criticized by many scholars was the tax benefits arising from the interest expense tax deductions stemming from the debt raised to finance the transaction. Tax deductibility of the interest on the new loans constitutes a major tax shield increasing the pre-transaction value, especially for firms with significant positive cash flows from operations. Clearly, the extent to which tax benefits can play a role in the wealth gains in LBOs depends on the fiscal regime and the marginal tax rates a company is subject to. Although the tax savings hypothesis seems to find support in the US LBO market (e.g., Kaplan 1989b; Schipper and Smith 1991; Kieschnick 1998; Halpern et al. 1999; Kosedag and Lane 2002), its relevance as driving motivation for LBOs is highly questioned by many authors.

First, the fact that tax benefits will give rise to higher post-LBO cash flows does not imply that it may constitute a true motive to go private. Indeed, in a competitive market for corporate control, the predictable and obtainable tax benefits will be appropriated by the pre-buyout investors, leaving no tax-related incentives for the post-buyout investors to take a company private. Kaplan (1989b) indeed shows that the total tax shield paid out as a premium to those investors selling out ranges from 21% to 142.6% of the premium depending on the marginal tax rate. This corroborates the intuition that tax benefits may also be conspicuous but the extent to which they represent the fueling reason of the transaction is disputable and largely depends on how much of those savings are appropriated by the target firm's shareholders (Renneboog and Simons 2005).

Second, Lowenstein (1985) and Frankfurter and Gunay (1993) criticize this source of gains from two perspectives. On the one hand, they claim that it overwhelms the other potential gains from LBOs and should therefore be restricted by governments. On the other hand, it only represents a wealth transfer from the state to older, inefficient firms that would therefore be subsidized by the government.

Third, the increase in leverage, among other things, carries with it some increase in the probability of default. Lenders' perceptions of this increase will be captured in the portion of the interest rate that is attributable to the default or risk premium. If the firm defaults, interest is neither paid nor deductible (and the firm is probably in a loss position anyway). The presence of large risk premiums means that interest deductions using the stated interest rate overstate the amount that is effectively tax deductible. The risk premium should be smaller if lenders perceive the debt is less risky because of the nature of the firm's expected cash flows or if the debt is well secured. All of this makes the true amount of tax savings more uncertain (Schipper and Smith 1991).

Fourth, personal tax treatment can affect the size of tax benefits (Miller 1977). When interest income has an unfavorable tax treatment compared to equity income, the corporate tax advantage may be canceled out. Moreover, the economic benefits of increased tax deductions from replacing equity with debt are affected by the incremental pretax (risk-adjusted) cost of debt versus equity capital in equilibrium arising from the unfavorable tax treatment of interest income. The different tax regimes across countries in terms of corporate and personal taxation may help explain why the tax motivation appears to be weakly supported outside the US (e.g., Weir et al. 2005). Finally, if tax advantages may be obtained by means of other leverage-increasing strategies such as leveraged recapitalizations, tax savings will no longer be an important reason for LBOs.

2.3.3 Redistribution Theories

Another theory regarding how LBO transactions create value for shareholders is that they expropriate value from non-equity stakeholders including bondholders, preferred stockholders, employees, government, and pension funds. There are three main mechanisms through which a firm can transfer wealth from bondholders to stockholders: (1) by an unexpected increase in the risk of investment projects; (2) by large increases in dividend payments, or (3) by an unexpected issue of debt of higher or equal seniority.

In LBO transactions, the third mechanism is likely to lead to substantial bondholder wealth expropriation, especially when the newly issued debt is not subordinated to the outstanding bonds and when it has a shorter duration. The value of existing bondholders' claims on the firm will be reduced if the firm engages in any one of these activities unless those bondholders have contractual protections (covenants) against the firm's actions. Covenants can protect bondholders in the event of changes of control, debt issues, and so on. In other words, the premium paid to the target firm's shareholders would not be due to the ability of post-LBO managers to increase firm value through better governance, efficiency improvements, and so on, but due to their inclination to shift wealth to shareholders from other stakeholders.

However, the bondholder wealth transfer motivation ignores some offsetting advantages that seemingly only benefit shareholders (Marais et al. 1989; Renneboog and Simons 2005). First, the value of the claims of other types of stakeholders (such as pensioners benefiting from corporate pension plans, employees benefiting from stock options, or fiscal authorities) may decline, thus offsetting the negative impact of increases in financial leverage. Second, the improved incentives deriving from high leverage and control concentration in the post-transaction firm may have a positive impact on the cash flow stream and consequently lead to further protection of the fixed payments to pre-transaction debtholders. Third, a buyout attempt by insiders may convey a favorable signal to financial markets about future returns, thereby raising expectations of the capability to service debt payments. Fourth, pre-transaction securities can be treated in a variety of ways during the transaction process: some are redeemed for cash, the others converted into other securities or renegotiated.

Another well-documented reason why shareholders can benefit from LBOs is wealth transfers from employees. Such transfers occur if firms breach their implicit contracts with employees by firing them, or renegotiating their contracts, as part of a post-LBO restructuring. This hypothesis, first proposed by Shleifer and Summers (1988), assumes that employees have an implicit, unwritten agreement with their firms who promise to provide them with long-term (lifetime) employment in exchange for lower wages. These agreements are breached if the company fires many of its workers after LBO. Moreover, workers are unable to recover these losses from the firm because these implicit agreements with their firms are legally unenforceable.

A case study is that of the acquisition of TWA by Carl Icahn in 1985. According to Shleifer and Summers (1988), the higher labor cost of TWA's workers reflected the firm-specific productivity developed by the employees. With deregulation, new airline entrants hired employees at much lower wages than unionized airlines such as TWA were paying. Consequently, investments made by employees to develop firm-specific skills are not paid their full value when previous labor contracts are broken by the new control group and there is a breach of trust.

However, these benefits are not likely to be large. First, such a breach would only generate a one-time gain because once it occurs the first time, workers will factor the non-enforceability of these implicit contracts into their future employment decisions which can raise turnover, increase hiring costs, and lower worker quality. Second, on average, LBOs do not result in job losses (e.g., Thompson and Wright 1995; Kaplan and Stromberg 2009). Furthermore, firing employees reduces a firm's production capacity and at some point lowers the quality and quantity of output because too few employees are involved in the production process. In contrast with this interpretation, if the higher salaries reflect union power resulting in monopoly rents to employees, then wage adjustments do not represent a breach of trust. They represent a movement from monopoly elements to competitive elements in the industry. If management inefficiency is involved, the introduction of efficient managers moves the industry from inefficiency to efficiency gains.

According to Lowenstein (1985), tax savings are also a form of expropriation from the state to shareholders in the sense that LBOs may generate a loss in tax revenues to the government because of the tax deductibility of interest expense the firm has to pay on the debt raised during the transaction. This loss would represent a sort of public subsidy to shareholders, therefore supporting any law or regulation aimed at cutting the amount of tax gains that can be earned through LBOs.

Another form of redistribution affects pension funds. When a firm executes an LBO, it often eliminates overfunded pensions and increases the default risk associated with its pension liabilities (Pontiff et al. 1990). Extreme evidence of this redistribution is that in the US, bankrupt firms are given the possibility to shift pension funds to the Pension Benefit Guaranty Corporation (PBGC). For example, Wilbur L. Ross and its subsidiaries purchased the assets of five steel producers including Bethlehem Steel and LTV Corporation to form the International Steel Group (ISG) in 2001. Shortly thereafter, ISG went bankrupt and Ross Group shifted $14 billion in pensions to PBGC. The group was also able to shift more than $5.9 billion in retiree health-care costs to former workers and Medicare.

The last well-known wealth transfer to shareholders may come from customers since acquisition could allow the target industry to experience an undue concentration. The argument is that if fewer firms account for a substantial increase in an industry's sales, these firms will recognize the impact of their actions and policies on one another. This recognized interdependence will lead to a consideration of actions and reactions to changes in policy that will tend toward tacit collusion. However, it must be said that this wealth transfer is unlikely to occur in LBOs because the acquiring entity is generally a private equity firm that, at least initially, does not allow the acquired firm to merge with other firms in the sector.

2.3.4 *Asymmetric Information and Undervaluation*

In a context of information asymmetries between managers and public shareholders, the former can exploit their superior access to information on the firm's prospects in order to take advantage of temporarily depressed stock market prices. Managers can therefore time their purchase of the company to take it private so as to benefit from the firm's undervaluation. This strategy is typically pursued in MBOs where incumbent managers have a better understanding of the value of the firm than public shareholders. However, professional investors such as private equity firms can also be better informed about the firm's expected cash flows as a result of their potential links with current managers and their greater ability to understand the firm's prospects.

According to this theory, the premium paid in LBOs is the result of the managers or other large investors being more informed of the expected firm value. Consequently, a buyout bid could represent a signal to the market that the company's future cash flows are higher than previously expected or that the firm is less risky than perceived by the public. Undervaluation could also be a consequence of strategies put into effect by managers to artificially depress the stock price.

For example, managers may adopt a selective disclosure policy in the firm's financial reporting by predating bad news before implementing the transaction and postponing good news until after the transaction is completed. A related signaling story is that financial leverage increases can convey positive management's expectations about the firm's prospects (Ross 1977; Leland and Pyle 1977; Heinkel 1982). According to these models, managers are assumed to possess better information than investors on the "intrinsic" value of the firm. Assuming that it is too costly for relatively low-value firms to give a wrong signal, these models suggest that the firms' capital structure decisions serve as valid signals that lead investors to correctly distinguish bad-quality from good-quality firms. In the context of these models, the unanticipated increase in financial leverage associated with a going-private buyout conveys positive information on the firm's future earnings prospects and thus results in an increase in the firm's stock price (Masulis 1983).

2.4 Going Dark: Mechanisms and Motivations

In a typical going private transaction, existing shareholders are cashed out by a subject who purchases outstanding shares by means of some form of tender offer. After that, the firm files with the SEC and the exchange (NYSE, NASDAQ, etc.) for deregistration under Section 12(b) and (g) of the Securities Exchange Act of 1934, thereby stopping periodic reporting obligations. Shares therefore cease to be traded.

A going dark deal is easier. First, there is no stock purchase. The firm simply deregisters with the SEC and the exchange by filing the required documents. Second, firms going dark continue to have shares publicly traded on "unofficial" markets such as the Pink Sheets or other OTC markets that do not require firms to report periodically. Third, unlike buyouts, shareholder approval is not necessary and the board of directors is in charge of the final decision regarding the transaction. However, some going dark transactions result from the firm not being able to meet the exchange's listing requirements. In this case, the board of directors chooses to go dark in response to an initiative by the stock exchange officials.

But what if the firm is not eligible for deregistration? We have seen that the issuer has to certify to the SEC on Form 15 that the class of securities is held of record by less than 300 persons or less than 500 persons, where the issuer's total assets have not exceeded $10 million on the last day of each of the issuer's most recent three fiscal years. Despite what may be thought, these conditions are quite easy to obtain even in firms with thousands of stockholders. In fact, the rapid dematerialization of shares as part of the SEC's effort to increase the efficiency of US stock trading, brokerage, and clearing has resulted in a dramatic decrease in the number of shareholders holding paper share certificates. Instead, they hold their claims in electronic form with the brokerage firms (the so-called shareholders of record). This is important because it is the number of shareholders of record, rather than the number of beneficial shareholders, that is used by the SEC to determine whether the number of shareholders is below 300. If the above conditions are not satisfied, the firm may however undertake a reverse stock split to reduce the number of outstanding shares below that threshold. In this case, a shareholder approval may be required depending on the state corporate law and a company's articles of incorporation.

2.4.1 Motives

Although going dark transactions share many of the motivations discussed above for the PTP deals, their completion is also motivated by some specific reasons. First of all, given that going dark firms are no longer required to meet periodic reporting obligations with the SEC and the exchange, they are sought by firms that consider compliance with SEC reporting and governance requirements to be excessively expensive. Not surprisingly, the financial press and academic studies (e.g., Marosi and Massoud 2007; Leuz et al. 2008; Panchapagesan and Werner 2004) found a significant trend of these transactions after the passage of the SOX that increased direct and indirect listing costs significantly. Going dark transactions can be of interest to firms with poor growth opportunities. They do not need substantial outside financing therefore reducing the value of having better access to external debt and equity capital given by the listing.

Another factor that can increase the probability of going dark is insider ownership. Larger managerial ownership can be exploited to act against shareholders' interests by taking the firm dark, reducing the responsibility and monitoring of executives by market and regulatory authorities, and increasing the risks of expropriation. Insider ownership is likely to interact with the ability of the firm to generate high operating cash flows. Unlike LBOs, going dark transactions do not increase a firm's leverage and consequently companies that end up being taken dark incur high free cash flow problems after the deal that could be exacerbated by entrenched managers. Likewise, a reduced presence of institutional shareholders in a firm's ownership structure may increase the probability of going dark as a consequence of a lower incentive to have the firm subject to the SEC's stricter governance and disclosure regulation.

Managers of firms that bear high information asymmetry could choose to go dark to take advantage of their private information regarding the firm value, thereby profiting from market misevaluation.

Official stock exchanges provide the firm with higher stock liquidity and visibility. As a result, going dark decisions are less likely when shares of the firms are actively traded and have experienced good price performance up to that moment.

Although LBOs normally target firms with a relatively prudent capital structure and then load them with debt, going dark may conversely affect already leveraged firms that use the strategy to preserve cash required to pay off debts and/or commit themselves to restructuring plans without market pressure and without wasting the time needed to comply with the SEC requirements.

In light of the above discussion, the decision to go dark could be moved by an aim either to increase or decrease shareholders' wealth depending on which motivation prevails. In general, whenever a deal appears to be determined by a managers' desire to rely on private information at the expense of shareholders, the market should react negatively to going dark announcements. Otherwise, a positive response can be expected. Macey et al. (2008) also find that stocks which moved from the NYSE to the Pink Sheets faced a significant increase in the bid-ask spread and poor market-adjusted returns over the first 60 trading days.

2.5 The Choice to Move from Main Markets to Second Markets

A related but different phenomenon is a firm's decision to transfer its listing from a main market to a second market, that is, a trading venue that shares legal and trading systems with the main market but maintains more relaxed listing requirements as well as governance and periodic disclosure obligations. Although this strategic choice is quite uncommon, there has been a marked increase in this trend from 2001 to 2006 among UK firms that switched from the London Stock Exchange (LSE) Main Market to LSE Alternative Investment Market (AIM). According to Vismara et al. (2012), since 1995, 282 firms had moved from the main market to AIM and 77% of these transfers occurred between 2001 and 2006.

Jenkinson and Ramadorai (2013) have analyzed some press releases of firms that chose to switch from the LSE Main Market to LSE AIM and found that the most common motivations supporting the choice are (1) a desire to avoid an undue regulatory burden and take advantage of the greater flexibility allowed by the AIM, (2) the possibility to share with other growth firms the same trading venue with positive externalities in terms of visibility and investor attention and financial support, (3) the possibility for foreign firms to be included in specific market indexes given that they are normally not allowed to be part of FTSE indexes in the main market, (4) the more attractive fiscal regime for UK investors in AIM firms.

The same authors also find that firms announcing a transfer from the main market to AIM experience in the three-week period around the announcement a negative cumulative abnormal return of 4.3%, which is not however statistically significant. The announcement could signal negative information about the firm in terms of poorer future corporate governance and market liquidity.

Despite the fact that announcement returns are negative, stock returns in the year following the transfer are significantly positive: they find a cumulative average abnormal return of about 25%. More interestingly, both authors try to explain these trends and find that they are not related to the effect of switching firms being excluded from one index and included in another that could result in negative returns at the time of exclusion when switching and subsequent positive returns after the inclusion in the new index. They are not even related to changes in ownership structure which tends to be stable over time. Instead, they appear to be related to post-switching operating performance: the EBITDA to total asset ratio increased from 1.4% as can be seen in the last financial report before the transfer to 8.8% on average 2 years later. If this operating performance improvement had been anticipated by the market at the time of the announcement, they would have observed a positive price reaction, but this is not the case. The market is likely to form its expectations gradually as new information on accounting performance becomes available.

Vismara et al. (2012) focus on the evolution of corporate governance characteristics around the passage and find that they weaken for switching firms. Compared to AIM firms that did not switch, they had a significantly larger number of directors 3 years before the transfer that decreased over time. They find the same trend for the number of non-executive directors. This means that transferring firms seem to get ready in advance of the future move by getting close to AIM firms' less stringent corporate governance.

References

Acharya, V. V., Franks, J., & Servaes, H. (2007). Private equity: Boom and bust? *Journal of Applied Corporate Finance, 19*(4), 1–10.

Acharya, V. V., Kehoe, C., & Reyner, M. (2009). Private equity vs. PLC boards in the UK: A comparison of practices and effectiveness. *Journal of Applied Corporate Finance, 21*(1), 45–56.

Ahern, K. R., & Weston, J. F. (2007, Spring/Summer). M&As: The good, the bad, and the ugly. *Journal of Applied Finance, 17*(1), 5–20.

Bebchuk, L., & Fried, J. (2004). *Pay without performance. The unfulfilled promise of executive compensation*. Cambridge, MA: Harvard University Press.

Berger, P. G., & Ofek, E. (1995). Diversification's effect on firm value. *Journal of Financial Economics, 37*(1), 39–65.

Campa, J. M., & Kedia, S. (2002). Explaining the diversification discount. *The Journal of Finance, 57*(4), 1731–1762.

DeAngelo, H., & DeAngelo, L. (1985). Managerial ownership of voting rights: A study of public corporations with dual classes of common stock. *Journal of Financial Economics, 14*(1), 33–69.

Easterbrook, F. H., & Fischel, D. R. (1982). Corporate control transactions. *Yale Law Journal, 91*(4), 698–737.

Frankfurter, G. M., & Gunay, E. (1993). Management buyouts and anticipated gains to shareholders—Theory and testing. *International Review of Financial Analysis, 2*(1), 33–50.

Galai, D., & Masulis, R. W. (1976). The option pricing model and the risk factor of stock. *Journal of Financial Economics, 3*(1–2), 53–81.

Halpern, P., Kieschnick, R., & Rotenberg, W. (1999). On the heterogeneity of leveraged going private transactions. *The Review of Financial Studies, 12*(2), 281–309.

Harris, M., & Raviv, A. (1990). Capital structure and the informational role of debt. *Journal of Finance, 45*(2), 321–349.

Heinkel, R. (1982). A theory of capital structure relevance under imperfect information. *The Journal of Finance, 37*(5), 1141–1150.

Holmstrom, B., & Kaplan, S. N. (2001). Corporate governance and merger activity in the United States: Making sense of the 1980s and 1990s. *Journal of Economic Perspectives, 15*(2), 121–144.

Jenkinson, T., & Ramadorai, T. (2013). Does one size fit all? The consequences of switching markets with different regulatory standards. *European Financial Management, 19*(5), 852–886.

Jensen, M. C. (1986). Agency costs of free cash flow, corporate finance, and takeovers. *The American Economic Review, 76*(2), 323–329.

Jensen, M. C. (1989, September–October). Eclipse of the public corporation. *Harvard Business Review*, 61–74.

Jensen, M. C., & Meckling, W. H. (1976). Theory of the firm: Managerial behavior, agency costs and ownership structure. *Journal of Financial Economics, 3*(4), 305–360.

Kaplan, S. N. (1989a). The effects of management buyouts on operating performance and value. *Journal of Financial Economics, 24*(2), 217–254.

Kaplan, S. N. (1989b). Management buyouts: Evidence on taxes as a source of value. *The Journal of Finance, 44*(3), 611–632.

Kaplan, S. N. (1991). The staying power of leveraged buyouts. *Journal of Financial Economics, 29*(2), 287–313.

Kaplan, S. N., & Stromberg, P. (2009). Leveraged buyouts and private equity. *Journal of Economic Perspectives, 23*(1), 121–146.

Kieschnick, R. L. (1998). Free cash flow and stockholder gains in going private transactions revisited. *Journal of Business Finance & Accounting, 25*(1–2), 187–202.

Kosedag, A., & Lane, W. R. (2002). Is it free cash flow, tax savings, or neither? An empirical confirmation of two leading going-private explanations: The case of ReLBOs. *Journal of Business Finance & Accounting, 29*(1–2), 257–271.

Lang, L. H., & Stulz, R. M. (1994). Tobin's q, corporate diversification, and firm performance. *Journal of Political Economy, 102*(6), 1248–1280.

Leland, H. E., & Pyle, D. H. (1977). Informational asymmetries, financial structure, and financial intermediation. *The Journal of Finance, 32*(2), 371–387.

Leuz, C., Triantis, A., & Wang, T. Y. (2008). Why do firms go dark? Causes and economic consequences of voluntary SEC deregistrations. *Journal of Accounting and Economics, 45*(2–3), 181–208.

Lowenstein, L. (1985). Management buyouts. *Columbia Law Review, 85*(4), 730–784.

Macey, J., O'Hara, M., & Pompilio, D. (2008). Down and out in the stock market: The law and economics of the delisting process. *The Journal of Law and Economics, 51*(4), 683–713.

Marais, L., Schipper, K., & Smith, A. (1989). Wealth effects of going private for senior securities. *Journal of Financial Economics, 23*(1), 155–191.

Marosi, A., & Massoud, N. (2007). Why do firms go dark? *Journal of Financial and Quantitative Analysis, 42*(2), 421–442.

Masulis, R. W. (1983). The impact of capital structure change on firm value: Some estimates. *The Journal of Finance, 38*(1), 107–126.

Masulis, R. W., & Thomas, R. S. (2009). Does private equity create wealth? The effects of private equity and derivatives on corporate governance. *The University of Chicago Law Review, 76*(1), 219–259.

Metrick, A., & Yasuda, A. (2010). The economics of private equity funds. *The Review of Financial Studies, 23*(6), 2303–2341.

Miller, M. H. (1977). Debt and taxes. *Journal of Finance, 32*(2), 261–275.

Morresi, O., & Pezzi, A. (2014). *Cross-border mergers and acquisitions. Theory and empirical evidence*. Houndmills: Palgrave Macmillan.

Panchapagesan, V., & Werner, I. M. (2004). *From pink slips to pink sheets: Market quality around delisting from Nasdaq*. EFA 2004 Maastricht meeting paper no. 4572. Available at https://papers.ssrn.com/sol3/papers.cfm?abstract_id=565325

Perotti, E. C., & Spier, K. E. (1993). Capital structure as a bargaining tool: The role of leverage in contract renegotiation. *The American Economic Review, 83*(5), 1131–1141.

Pontiff, J., Shleifer, A., & Weisbach, M. S. (1990). Reversions of excess pension assets after takeovers. *The RAND Journal of Economics, 21*(4), 600–613.

Rajan, R., Servaes, H., & Zingales, L. (2000). The cost of diversity: The diversification discount and inefficient investment. *The Journal of Finance, 55*(1), 35–80.

Rappaport, A. (1990). The staying power of the public corporation. *Harvard Business Review, 68*(1), 96–104.

Renneboog, L., & Simons, T. (2005). Public-to-private transactions: LBOs, MBOs, MBIs and IBOs. *European Corporate Governance Institute*, Finance working paper no. 94.

Ross, S. A. (1977). The determination of financial structure: The incentive-signalling approach. *The Bell Journal of Economics, 8*(1), 23–40.

Schipper, K., & Smith, A. (1991). Effects of management buyouts on corporate interest and depreciation tax deductions. *Journal of Law and Economics, 34*(2), 295–341.

Scholes, M. S., & Wolfson, M. A. (1990). The effects of changes in tax laws on corporate reorganization activity. *Journal of Business, 63*(1), 141–164.

Shleifer, A., & Summers, L. H. (1988). Breach of trust in hostile takeovers. In A. J. Auerbach (Ed.), *Corporate takeovers: Causes and consequences* (pp. 33–68). Chicago: University of Chicago Press.

Shleifer, A., & Vishny, R. W. (1991). The takeover wave of the 1980s. *Journal of Applied Corporate Finance, 4*(3), 49–56.

Strömberg, P. (2007). *The new demography of private equity.* Swedish Institute for Financial Research, Stockholm School of Economics, CEPR and NBER, working paper.

Thompson, S., & Wright, M. (1995). Corporate governance: The role of restructuring transactions. *The Economic Journal, 105*(430), 690–703.

Travlos, N. G., & Cornett, M. M. (1993). Going private buyouts and determinants of shareholders' returns. *Journal of Accounting, Auditing & Finance, 8*(1), 1–25.

Venanzi, D. (2012). *Financial performance measures and value creation: The state of the art.* Heidelberg: Springer Science & Business Media.

Villalonga, B. (2004a). Does diversification cause the "diversification discount"? *Financial Management, 33*(2), 5–27.

Villalonga, B. (2004b). Diversification discount or premium? New evidence from the business information tracking series. *The Journal of Finance, 59*(2), 479–506.

Vismara, S., Paleari, S., & Ritter, J. R. (2012). Europe's second markets for small companies. *European Financial Management, 18*(3), 352–388.

Weir, C., Laing, D., & Wright, M. (2005). Incentive effects, monitoring mechanisms and the market for corporate control: An analysis of the factors affecting public to private transactions in the UK. *Journal of Business Finance and Accounting, 32*(5–6), 909–943.

Wright, M., Renneboog, L., Simons, T., & Scholes, L. (2006). Leveraged buyouts in the UK and Continental Europe: Retrospect and prospect. *Journal of Applied Corporate Finance, 18*(3), 38–55.

CHAPTER 3

The Decision to Delist: International Empirical Evidence

Barbara Fidanza

3.1 Introduction

Over the last 20 years, the empirical literature has paid a great deal of attention to firms' delisting decisions, commonly defined as "going private transactions" (GPT) or "public-to-private" (PTP) operations.

Some studies state that in Europe, GPTs increased in the years prior to the crisis, up until 2011 (Renneboog et al. 2007; Thomsen and Vinten 2014; Croci and Del Giudice 2014). Gao et al. (2013) and Grullon et al. (2015) show that the reduction in the number of firms listed in the US is a trend that began in 1996. Doidge et al. (2013) show that this reduction in initial public offerings (IPOs) was accompanied by a rapid increase in delisting operations, widening the gap between the number of new quotations and delisted firms.

Martinez and Serve (2017) analyze the phenomenon with reference to 42 countries in the period 2008–2012 with 75% of the phenomenon being concentrated in three geographical areas: US, UK and Europe. As far as a comparison between the percentage of companies delisted from the stock exchange and that of new listings is concerned, the most significant gap occurs in the US and the UK with a positive differential of the former toward the latter of 6.2% and 7.6% respectively. In Europe, the gap is inverse, but less important: new quotations exceed delistings by 0.4%.

B. Fidanza et al., *The Decision to Delist from the Stock Market*,
https://doi.org/10.1007/978-3-319-95049-5_3

Macey et al. (2008) distinguish involuntary delisting from voluntary delisting. In the first case, the company is involuntarily forced to cancel itself from the stock exchange due to non-compliance with regulatory requirements or because the company incurs bankruptcy/liquidation. Voluntary delistings are, on the other hand, a consequence of managerial choice and in this specific case, we refer to the concept of GPTs. GPTs are heterogeneous. They can lead to simultaneous delisting from all lists (domestic or otherwise) without subsequent trading, or to cancelation from a market, but with trading maintained on less regulated stock exchanges or other markets.

When the cancelation from all stock exchanges is simultaneous, the transactions can differ in relation to the firm's ownership structure. For companies with diffused ownership, the substantial change in corporate control is a necessary condition for delisting and frequently transactions are carried out through the participation of institutional investors (private equity), very often in the form of an LBO. Leuz et al. (2008) refer to operations in which ownership is concentrated, with few investors who have no interest in trading their stocks on the market. For companies with a concentrated ownership structure, the control change can be of a different kind and the minority shareholders are forced out of the company through mergers and acquisitions. DeAngelo et al. (1984) define these operations as "buyout transactions with minority freeze-outs" (BOSO) in which the ownership is concentrated and can decide, therefore, to delist from the stock exchange. In these transactions, the majority shareholders use their rights to purchase the shares of minority shareholders. In Europe, most GPTs take place via BOSO because they have been regulated and also encouraged by the Thirteen Directive on Takeovers.[1]

When companies are canceled from a stock exchange, but continue to be traded in another (foreign, less regulated, or not regulated at all), the transaction is called "going dark" or "deregistration". It is not a real delisting but a form of delisting that describes a step down in the firm's quotation cycle. In this case, a change in corporate control is not necessary. The companies seeking deregistration bring the number of shareholders down to below 300 because in the US, in companies with fewer than 300 shareholders, the decision to delist the firm is only taken by the board of directors (Marosi and Massoud 2007; Leuz et al. 2008; see Sect. 1.3 for a detailed discussion of delisting regulation in the US).

[1] Directive on takeover bids (Directive 2004/25/EC of the European Parliament and the Council of 21 April 2004).

This chapter aims to review the empirical literature on the topic by analyzing 40 studies, mainly published in the last 20 years, and the intention is to give a synoptic view that is as complete as possible by referring to the methodological aspects of empirical tests, the hypotheses, and their consistency with the results obtained.

There are essentially three streams of empirical literature on delisting. The first one studies, in voluntary delisting the link between the decision to undertake the operation and the determinants in accordance with the different theoretical models (see Sect. 1.4 for these models). These determinants mainly pertain to the firm's financial structure and performance characteristics, business characteristics, and stock liquidity. The other two strands highlight the reasons that lead to involuntary delisting and study the effects of delisting on firm value.

With reference to this general framework, the chapter is organized as described below.

Section 3.2 takes into account the empirical methodologies adopted in the studies examined, as well as their size in terms of geographical coverage and time period of analysis. Subsequent sections analyze the main results. For voluntary delistings, we distinguish them according to determinants and the aim is to quantify the robustness of the hypotheses that have obtained more robust empirical evidence (Sect. 3.3). The last two sections provide a summary of the studies that have investigated the reasons for involuntary delisting and the impact of delisting on a firm's value.

3.2 Methodological Aspects

Table 3.1 shows the 40 studies analyzed (one panel for each literature strand) and divides them into methodology (first column), objectives (second column), sample, reference market, and time period under investigation in the remaining columns.

The geographical coverage of empirical tests is mainly US (26 studies), followed by Europe (6 studies) and UK (6 studies). In the remaining studies, the analysis is conducted by comparing the results in different countries. Considering the time span, the samples cover a wide period, from 1965 to 2011.

Some clarification on the methodological aspects is required for a better understanding of the results that will be discussed.

Fourteen studies (mainly belonging to the first strand) are conducted by logit regressions; the reference model generally takes the following form:

Table 3.1 Empirical literature for each research stream

Methodology	*Objectives*	*Study*	*Sample*	*Country*	*Years*
Panel A—voluntary delisting					
Logit regression	GPT determinants	Achleitner et al. (2013)	115 LBOs+ control group	Europe	1997–2007
		Aslan and Kumar (2011)	274 GPTs+ control group	USA	1996–2006
		Martinez and Serve (2011)	70 freeze-outs+ control group	France	1997–2006
		Opler and Titman (1993)	180 LBOs + control group	USA	1980–1990
		Kashefi Pour and Lasfer (2013)	158 GPTs + 26 going dark + control group	UK	1995–2009
		Weir et al. (2005a)	95 LBOs + control group	UK	1998–2000
		Weir et al. (2005b)	84 LBOs + control group	UK	1998–2000
		Weir and Wright (2006)	96 LBOs + 258 acquisitions of listed firms	UK	1998–2000
		Weir et al. (2008)	115 GPTs+ control group	USA	1998–2001
	GPT determinants + going dark determinants + SOX effects	Leuz et al. (2008)	484 going dark+436 GPTs+ control group	USA	1998–2004
	GPT determinants + SOX effects	Engel et al. (2007)	237 GPTs + control group	USA	1998–2005
Difference between the value of the determinants for delisted firms and non-delisted firms	GPT determinants	Bharath and Dittmar (2010)	1023 GPTs + control group	USA	1980–2004
		Kim and Lyn (1991)	53 LBOs + control group	USA	1976–1984

Cox's proportional hazard model	GPT determinants	Kashefi Pour and Lasfer (2013)	158 GPTs + 26 going dark + control group	UK	1995–2009
		Mehran and Peristiani (2010)	262 GPTs+ control group	USA	1990–2007
Panel B—involuntary delisting					
Logit regression	Link between delisting and financial performance	Li and Zhou (2006)	3.898 firms listed (1.621 delisting) on AMEX	USA	1980–1999
		Seguin and Smoller (1997)	5.896 firms listed on NASDAQ	USA	1974–1998
	Link between delisting and the violation of minimum requirements	Harris et al. (2008)	1.098 firms delisted from NASDAQ	USA	1999–2002
Difference between survival/death rates in samples and sub-samples discriminated by determinants	Link between delisting and financial performance	Baker and Kennedy (2002)	7.455 firms listed on NYSE and AMEX (4.118 delisting)	USA	1965–1995
		Fama and French (2004)	NYSE and AMEX firms	USA	1980–2001
		Gerakos et al. (2013)	1.461 firms delisted from AIM, LSE and NASDAQ	USA+UK	1995–2008
		Peristiani and Hong (2004)	9.095 firms listed on NYSE, AMEX, NASDAQ	USA	1992–2002
	Link between delisting and investor type	Bhattacharya et al. (2015)	37.863 listed firms	USA	1985–2006
	Link between delisting and stock exchange regulation	Cattaneo et al. (2015)	299 listed firms	Italy	1861–2011

(*continued*)

Table 3.1 (continued)

Methodology	*Objectives*	*Study*	*Sample*	*Country*	*Years*
Performance comparison in samples and sub-samples discriminated by market type	Link between delisting and stock exchange regulation	Serrano (2013)	234 firms delisted from NYSE and TSX	USA+ Canada	2002–2009
Exploratory survey	Link between delisting and the violation of minimum requirements	Chen and Schoderbek (1999)	295 firms delisted from AMEX	USA	1981–1992
Cox's proportional hazard model	Link between delisting and financial performance	Wagner and Cockburn (2010)	356 firms delisted from NASDAQ	USA	1998–2001
Event study + OLS between CARs and determinants	Link between delisting and the violation of minimum requirements	Sanger and Peterson (1990)	520 firms delisted from NYSE, AMEX and NASDAQ	USA	1962–1985
Panel C—effects of delisting on firm value					
Event study	Effect of delisting on shareholder wealth	Andres et al. (2007)	115 LBOs	Europe	1997–2005
		Geranio and Zanotti (2012)	106 GPTs	Europe	2000–2005
		Leuz et al. (2008)	484 deregistrations+436 GPTs	USA	1998–2004
		Marosi and Massoud (2007)	177 LBOs	UK	1997–2003
Analysis of quoted spread: average daily closing ask-closing bid divided by the closing mid-quote	Effect of delisting on shareholder wealth + determinants	Angel et al. (2004)	1.098 involuntary delistings from NASDAQ	USA	1975–2005
	Effect of delisting on shareholder wealth	Harris et al. (2008)	1.098 firms delisted from NASDAQ	USA	1999–2002

Event study+OLS between CARs and determinants	Effect of delisting on shareholder wealth + role of corporate control	Croci and Del Giudice (2014)	429 GPTs	UK + Europe	1999–2005
	Effect of delisting on shareholder wealth + link between delisting and the violation of minimum requirements	Sanger and Peterson (1990)	520 involuntary delistings from NYSE, AMEX and NASDAQ	USA	1962–1985
	Effect of delisting on shareholder wealth + determinants	Angel et al. (2004)	1.098 involuntary delistings from NASDAQ	USA	1975–2005
		Renneboog et al. (2007)	177 LBOs	UK	1997–2003
Analysis of premium between offer price and pre-delisting market price + OLS between premium and determinants	Effect of delisting on shareholder wealth + determinants	Bajo et al. (2013)	85 freeze-outs	Europe	1998–2012
Event study + analysis of premium between offer price and pre-delisting market price	Effect of delisting on shareholder wealth	Boubaker et al. (2014)	314 GPTs	Europe	1997–2011
		DeAngelo et al. (1984)	81 GPTs	USA	1973–1980
		Kaplan (1989a, b)	76 MBOs	USA	1980–1986
		Lehn and Poulsen (1989)	263 LBOs + control group	USA	1980–1987
		Sannajust (2010)	399 GPTs	Europe+ UK+USA	2000–2007
Momentum strategy test	Effect of delisting on shareholder wealth	Eisdorfer (2008)	Involuntary delistings from NYSE, AMEX and NASDAQ	USA	1975–2005

$$Y = a_0 + \sum_{i=1}^{n} a_i x_i + e$$

where Y is a binary variable taking value 1 if the firm is delisted, 0 otherwise, x_i is a vector of n independent variables, proxies for the factors drawn from the various theories, a_i is the regression coefficient for the variable i, a_0 and e are, respectively, the constant and error term. A positive regression coefficient indicates that when the independent variable increases, the probability of delisting increases.

In some studies (10 studies) the hypotheses are tested by observing the statistical significance of the difference between the value of the determinants calculated for the companies subject to delisting and the same calculated for the companies that remain public, or the statistical significance of the difference between the survival/death rates calculated on samples and sub-samples discriminated by each determinant.

In the strand of studies that tests the effect of delisting on firm value or in the one that investigates whether financial performance is also a determinant of the decision, the event study methodology is generally used (14 studies) or the premium between the offer price and the pre-delisting market price is compared and the statistical significance of the difference measured. Two works study the quality of stock by means of an analysis of quoted spread.[2]

In an event study, the focus is on the stock price reaction following the occurrence of a given event. In order to evaluate unusual trends, the abnormal returns (ARs), calculated as the current return minus the expected or estimated return, are used as a reference variable. For each share, the return has two components: the "normal" return (return that would have been achieved if the event had not occurred) and a disturbing term, able to measure the specific effect induced by the event. This means that[3]:

$$R_{it} = AR_{it} + \mathrm{E}(R_{it}),$$

[2] Quoted spread is the average daily closing ask-closing bid divided by the closing mid-quote.

[3] Most studies rely on these models to estimate normal returns: (a) index model; (b) comparison period return approach; (c) market model; (d) CAPM; (e) control portfolio model.

where R_{it} is the return of stock i in day t; AR_{it} is the daily abnormal return of stock i in day t (disturbing term); $E(R_{it})$ is the normal/expected return. In each day of the study period, the average abnormal return of the sample can be calculated as follows:

$$\overline{AR}_{it} = \frac{1}{M}\sum_{i=1}^{M} AR_{it}$$

where M is the number of companies in the sample. Abnormal returns are normally studied over a time period ($-N$ days; $+N$ days) centered on day 0, the event date. The length of the period depends on the accuracy of the event date: a greater accuracy in its definition justifies a shorter interval. However, in an efficient market, prices adjust according to future expectations on corporate policies; it is therefore difficult to identify the exact moment in which the market forms and changes these expectations. The price response to a business decision may not occur on the day of the announcement, but may occur even earlier if this decision is expected to be taken. This factor makes the study period larger. Possible anticipation effects must be considered in some way, to avoid underestimating the effect on the value due to the event announcement. One way to see if such a phenomenon has occurred is to study, in addition to daily abnormal returns, the cumulative abnormal returns ($CARs$), expressed as:

$$CAR_t = \sum_{t=-N}^{+N} \overline{AR}_{it}.$$

Three studies apply specific methodologies: Sanger and Peterson (1990), Mehran and Peristiani (2010) and Kashefi Pour and Lasfer (2013), in addition to traditional techniques, also apply the Cox's proportional hazard model through which, when explaining the determinants of the delisting, they are able to analyze their variability within the entire quotation cycle of the company which therefore becomes also discriminating. Eisdorfer (2008) makes an important contribution and adopts a test on the momentum strategy.[4]

[4] The momentum strategy assumes that stocks with good performance in the past will have the same results in the future and vice versa. The strategy is therefore to buy stocks that have been highly profitable over the past 9–12 months and sell those with low performance.

3.3 Determinants of Voluntary Delisting

The most frequently used determinants in the first stream of empirical studies are analyzed below. For each one, we describe the methods used to measure them, as well as the sign of the link hypothesized by the theories, and consider the empirical results for the expected sign. Table 3.2 contains this analysis. For each determinant (first column), the model and expected sign of the determinant-delisting link are indicated and the last three columns show the most commonly used proxies for each determinant and the main results (sign and statistical significance) of the studies. It should be noted that the same variable can be a proxy for several determinants.

This synoptic framework can be used to see which determinant is more robust.

3.3.1 Free Cash Flow

The free cash flow (FCF) hypothesis by Jensen (1986, 1989) is useful when explaining delisting. If the available liquidity is used for projects with negative NPV or for an excessive consumption of private benefits, rather than for distributing dividends to shareholders, the resulting value loss can be defined as an agency cost of equity because it is caused by potential conflicts between managers, who should pursue the interests of shareholders but do not always do so, and the shareholders. As a result, companies with high FCFs suffer higher agency costs of equity; if the company is listed, control over potential moral hazard behavior is more difficult and managerial discretion is wider. In this context, going private involves benefits, especially if this occurs through an LBO: the debt reduces wasted liquidity because cash flows must also be used for debt payments and managers therefore know that they cannot use them freely.

With reference to the indirect costs of financial distress, value losses due to poor firm management with financial difficulties (Myers 1977, 1984) are lower when FCF is higher. This condition often concerns mature companies with few growth opportunities and which prefer the status of private firms.

For both aspects, high FCFs make delisting operations more likely.

With regard to this determinant, the empirical results are not univocal and give little support to its importance: the determinant is statistically significant in only 3 studies out of 13 and positive signs prevail over negative ones and always concern the US market. Leuz et al. (2008) show

Table 3.2 The determinants of voluntary delisting

	Theoretical model		Empirical studies		
Determinants	**Model**	**Relationship: expected sign**[a]	**Proxies**	**Study**	**Relationship: obtained sign**[a]
Free cash flow	Agency (FCF problems)	+	EBITDA/market value	Weir et al. (2008)	–
			EBITDA/sales	Engel et al. (2007)	+
				Mehran and Peristiani (2010)	+
				Weir et al. (2005a)	–
				Weir and Wright (2006)	+
			EDITDA/total assets	Bharath and Dittmar (2010)	+
				Leuz et al. (2008)	+
			EDITDA/total assets	Achleitner et al. (2013)	–
	Costs of financial distress	+	FCF/total assets	Kashefi Pour and Lasfer (2013)	–
			Std. dev. (EBITDA/total assets), last 5 years	Achleitner et al. (2013)	–
			(Net income+depreciation)/sales	Kim and Lyn (1991)	+
			(Three-year average FCF)/sales	Weir et al. (2005b)	–
			(EBIT-capital expenditures – net working capital investment)/total assets	Aslan and Kumar (2011)	+
Diversification	Agency	+	[illegible] where si is the % of sales in the segment i	Opler and Titman (1993)	+
	Risks/costs of financial distress	+		Weir et al. (2008)	+

(*continued*)

Table 3.2 (continued)

Level of competition and growth opportunities	Agency (FCF problems)	−	FCF/enterprise value	Opler and Titman (1993)	−
			R&D/sales	Bharath and Dittmar (2010)	+
				Mehran and Peristiani (2010)	−
				Weir et al. (2008)	−
	Agency (monitoring problems)	+	Market to book value	Aslan and Kumar (2011)	−
				Bharath and Dittmar (2010)	−
				Kim and Lyn (1991)	−
				Mehran and Peristiani (2010)	+
	Agency (cost of debt)	−		Opler and Titman (1993)	−
				Weir et al. (2008)	−
			Market capitalization/total assets	Weir et al. (2005a)	−
	Asymmetric information	+	Total assets/(total assets−equity book value+equity market value)	Engel et al. (2007)	+
			Intangible assets/total assets	Kashefi Pour and Lasfer (2013)	+
			Sales growth rate over the two years prior to the acquisition	Weir and Wright (2006)	−
	Costs of financial distress	+/−	Sales growth rate over the year prior to the acquisition	Martinez and Serve (2011)	+
			Asset growth rate over the year prior to the acquisition	Leuz et al. (2008)	−
			Sales growth rate over the year prior to the acquisition	Weir et al. (2005b)	−
	Access to capital	−		Engel et al. (2007)	−
				Aslan and Kumar (2011)	−
			Five-year geometric average growth rate of sales	Kim and Lyn (1991)	−

Leverage and financial risk	Agency (monitoring)	–	Debt/total assets	Aslan and Kumar (2011)	–
				Bharath and Dittmar (2010)	+
				Engel et al. (2007)	+
				Kashefi Pour and Lasfer (2013)	+
	Risks/costs of financial distress	–		Kim and Lyn (1991)	–
				Leuz et al. (2008)	+
				Martinez and Serve (2011)	–
				Opler and Titman (1993)	–
	Access to capital	–		Weir et al. (2008)	–
			Debt/enterprise value	Achleitner et al. (2013)	–
			Long-term debt/market capitalization	Mehran and Peristiani (2010)	+
	Agency (cost of debt)	+	Ohlson distress score	Leuz et al. (2008)	+
			Beta	Martinez and Serve (2011)	–
			Yearly standard deviation of firm's stock returns	Mehran and Peristiani (2010)	+
Company size	Agency (FCF problems, monitoring problems)	+	ln(total assets)	Aslan and Kumar (2011)	–
				Leuz et al. (2008)	–
	Costs of financial distress	+		Marinez and Serve (2011)	–
				Opler and Titman (1993)	–
	Asymmetric information	–		Weir et al. (2005a)	–
				Weir and Wright (2006)	+
	Compliance cost	–	Total assets	Kim and Lyn (1991)	–
			ln(equity market value)	Kashefi Pour and Lasfer (2013)	–

(*continued*)

Table 3.2 (continued)

Ex-ante performance	Agency (FCF problems)	+	ROA	Aslan and Kumar (2011)	−
				Engel et al. (2007)	+
	Agency	−		Kashefi Pour and Lasfer (2013)	+
				Martinez and Serve (2011)	−
	Asymmetric information (adverse selection)	−		Opler and Titman (1993)	−
			Abnormal return with respect to the market index over the previous year	Mehran and Peristiani (2010)	−
				Weir et al. (2008)	−
	Risks/costs of financial distress	+	ln(annual stock return)	Leuz et al. (2008)	−
			Market capitalization over the previous year/market capitalization over the previous two years	Weir and Wright (2006)	−
	Compliance cost	−	Market capitalization/market capitalization over the previous year	Weir et al. (2005b)	−
			Market to book value	Martinez and Serve (2011)	−
Company age	Takeover defense	+	Age of firm	Aslan and Kumar (2011)	−
	Asymmetric information (adverse selection)	−		Opler and Titman (1993)	−
	Risks/costs of financial distress	+	Age of listing	Weir et al. (2008)	−
Taxation	Capital structure	+	Tax paid/sales	Mehran and Peristiani (2010)	−
				Weir et al. (2008)	+
			Three-year average tax paid/sales	Weir et al. (2005b)	+
			Tax paid/EBITDA	Achleitner et al. (2013)	−
			Tax paid/total assets	Engel et al. (2007)	+
			Tax rate	Achleitner et al. (2013)	+

Corporate governance quality	Agency (FCF problems, private benefits, monitoring)	–	% non-executive directors on the board	Weir et al. (2005a)	+
			% independent directors on the board	Weir et al. (2005a)	+
			% independent non-executive directors on the board	Weir and Wright (2006)	–
			Number of independent directors on the board	Leuz et al. (2008)	–
			Dummy=1 if a company has at least three non-executive directors or advisor, 0 otherwise	Weir and Wright (2006)	–
	Compliance cost	–	Dummy=1 if a company has at least three non-executive directors, 0 otherwise	Weir et al. (2005b)	–
			Dummy=1 if a company has at least three non-executive directors and the positions of CEO and chairman are separated, 0 otherwise	Weir et al. (2005b)	–
			Duality=1 if the positions of CEO and chairman are held by the same person, 0 otherwise	Weir and Wright (2006)	+
				Weir et al. (2005a)	+
				Weir et al. (2005b)	+
			Board size	Opler and Titman (1993)	+
Institutional investors	Agency (monitoring problems)	–	Total % of shareholding held by institutions that have at least a 3% stake	Weir et al. (2005b)	+
				Weir et al. (2005a)	+
			Total % of shareholding held by institutions	Bharath and Dittmar (2010)	–
	Asymmetric information	–	Number of analysts following the firm	Bharath and Dittmar (2010)	–
			% difference in the number of analysts	Mehran and Peristiani (2010)	+
			Dummy=1 if the firm has institutional ownership, 0 otherwise	Leuz et al. (2008)	–
Analyst coverage	Asymmetric information	–	Annual average of the monthly number of recommendations	Martinez and Serve (2011)	–
			Annual standard deviation of stock returns	Kashefi Pour and Lasfer (2013)	–
				Mehran and Peristiani (2010)	–
			Stock trading volume/market capitalization	Mehran and Peristiani (2010)	–

(continued)

Table 3.2 (continued)

Insider ownership and ownership concentration	Agency (private benefits)	−	Equity ownership held by board members	Engel et al. (2007)	+
				Weir et al. (2005b)	+
				Weir and Wright (2006)	+
	Agency (monitoring problems)	−		Weir et al. (2008)	−
			Equity ownership held by board members /outstanding shares	Kashefi Pour and Lasfer (2013)	+
			Equity ownership held by board members/total assets	Weir and Wright (2006)	−
			CEO's equity ownership	Weir et al. (2005a)	+
	Agency (cost of debt)	−	Sum of all first-tier voting stakes of the firm's professional executive manager	Achleitner et al. (2013)	−
			Dummy=0 if the majority ownership is held by individuals or families, 1 otherwise	Aslan and Kumar (2011)	−
	Takeover defense	+	% of voting rights held by the ultimate controlling shareholder	Achleitner et al. (2013)	−
			% of voting rights held by the ultimate controlling shareholder if it is a family, 0 otherwise	Achleitner et al. (2013)	−
	Asymmetric information (adverse selection)	+	% cash flow rights held by the ultimate controlling shareholder if it is not part of the management, and 0 otherwise	Achleitner et al. (2013)	−
Speculative pressure	Takeover defense	+	Dummy=1 if there had been press coverage of bid speculation in the period three months to 15 months prior to the acquisition, 0 otherwise	Weir and Wright (2006)	+
			Dummy=1 if there had been a failed hostile bid in one month prior to GPT announcement	Weir et al. (2005a)	+
			Dummy=1 if there had been a failed hostile bid in one month prior to GPT announcement	Weir et al. (2005b)	+
			Number of firms taken over in the same sector/ number of firms in the same sector	Weir and Wright (2006)	−

External financing needs	Access to capital	–	Net fixed assets/assets	Bharath and Dittmar (2010)	–
			Capital expenditures/total assets	Aslan and Kumar (2011)	–
				Kashefi Pour and Lasfer (2013)	–
				Martinez and Serve (2011)	–
				Mehran and Peristiani (2010)	–
				Weir and Wright (2006)	–
			Dummy=1 if a firm paid out dividends during the fiscal year, 0 otherwise	Bharath and Dittmar (2010)	–
			Market value/book value of equity	Kashefi Pour and Lasfer (2013)	–
Liquidity	Access to capital	–	Daily shares traded in past 12 months/outstanding shares	Bharath and Dittmar (2010)	–
				Engel et al. (2007)	–
				Kashefi Pour and Lasfer (2013)	–
			Daily shares traded in past 12 months	Kashefi Pour and Lasfer (2013)	–
			Daily shares traded in past 250-day window/outstanding shares	Achleitner et al. (2013)	–
			Change in the logarithm of shares traded in past 12 months	Leuz et al. (2008)	–
			log(annual average of the number of stocks traded in a given day in thousands of securities)	Martinez and Serve (2011)	–

[a](−) = greater value of the determinant, lower probability of delisting; (+) = greater value of the determinant, greater probability of delisting; the significant results are highlighted in gray

that delisted companies have lower FCFs than companies that remain on the market. Mehran and Peristiani (2010) and Bharath and Dittmar (2010) get opposite results. The latter, distinguishing two sub-periods, pre-1990 and post-1990, show that during the 1980s, companies with high FCFs more frequently started the going private transactions, but for the period from 1990 onwards, the trend is not so clear cut.

3.3.2 Diversification

The degree of diversification describes the risk aptitude of top management, its objectives, and its system of values. The determinant represents a strategic corporate variable which is clearly linked to risk: diversification lowers risk. Firms with diffused ownership will be characterized by a greater degree of diversification to reduce the non-systematic risk that cannot be offset at personal level. For these reasons, companies that delist will have more diversified activities than those that remain public since there is less risk of bankruptcy (Titman and Wessels 1988).

From the perspective of agency costs, the link between the determinant and the propensity to delist is the same; diversification is influenced by managers' personal interests which can be associated with managerial entrenchment, cross-subsidization or the desire to increase their reputation in order to demonstrate that management is able to manage a complex organization (Jensen 1986; Shleifer and Vishny 1992).

The only two studies that test this determinant achieve significant results that are consistent with expectations (Opler and Titman 1993; Weir et al. 2008).

3.3.3 Level of Competition and Growth Opportunities

The variable concerns the influence of product market and market factors on GPTs.

Jensen (1986) argues that the incentive for excessive use of FCF is greater when growth opportunities are lower. Fewer growth opportunities therefore increase the probability of delisting (negative link).

On the other hand (positive link), firms operating in highly competitive sectors where innovation is a strategy that determines business success and growth opportunities are higher tend to proceed more frequently with delisting. These firms suffer high agency costs related to the difficulties in monitoring the management's decision (Jensen and Meckling 1976) and greater information asymmetries (stock price is more volatile and less informative for companies with high growth opportunities): evaluating current assets is not the same as evaluating growth opportunities for which the drivers of future success are not known.

From the point of view of expected distress costs, the link between growth opportunities and the probability of GPTs is not univocal and can have more than one interpretation. Expected bankruptcy costs have a greater effect, so much so that they discourage delisting operations when the uniqueness of the business is greater and costs related to the loss of customers, suppliers, and workers are higher. This circumstance generally occurs for firms operating in sectors with low competition and growth opportunities (positive link). Myers (1977) states that if the distress risk is high, the value of growth opportunities is reduced, and the greater the incidence of growth opportunities on stock price, the higher the costs of expected distress. Delisting is more likely for companies with reduced growth opportunities (negative link).

Moreover, for a given stock price, when growth options are lower, the firm's value depends more on the value of tangible assets and collaterals for current and future creditors (lower agency costs of debt) as well as the ability to increase the debt in the future and proceed to an LBO are greater.

One of the benefits of listing is easier access to capital; growing companies with significant current and future investments that could be limited by the difficulty of obtaining loans if leverage is already high are those that most frequently access the markets (Kim and Weisbach 2008). In contrast, companies that do not have large investments and opportunities for future growth are more likely to want to get out (negative link).

The most commonly used proxy for growth opportunities at an empirical level is the market-to-book ratio at equity or company level. Even the level of competition/uniqueness of the product measured by the impact of research and development (R&D) and marketing costs can be useful for measuring the determinant: these expenses are generally lower for companies that compete in markets where there are few competitors and few growth opportunities. Some studies have investigated the link between the growth rates of sales or assets and delisting operations. In terms of results, the significant links are always negative, no matter which proxy is used: the fewer the growth opportunities, the greater the propensity to be removed from the public market (Mehran and Peristiani 2010; Bharath and Dittmar 2010; Weir et al. 2005a; Weir and Wright 2006; Leuz et al. 2008; Aslan and Kumar 2011; Kim and Lyn 1991).

3.3.4 *Leverage and Financial Risk*

Companies with low debt do not benefit from the monitoring by creditors of managerial discretion and as a result, agency costs are higher (Jensen and Meckling 1976). If the debt is reduced, the company has less distress risk and greater ability to contract debt in the future (required in LBOs). A low level of debt is associated with a greater probability of delisting. This negative link is confirmed by five studies (Aslan and Kumar 2011; Kim and Lyn 1991; Martinez and Serve 2011; Achleitner et al. 2013). For some authors, this would confirm the fact that staying in the market is important in terms of access to capital when the firm is already heavily leveraged.

Kashefi Pour and Lasfer (2013), Leuz et al. (2008) and Mehran and Peristiani (2010) find a positive and significant link between debt and delisting that they attribute to debt agency problems: managers could aim to expropriate wealth from creditors in favor of shareholders, favoring GPTs financed by debt, even when it is already high.

3.3.5 *Company Size*

The expected link between the size of the company and the propensity to delisting is generally positive. Agency problems tend to be more important in large companies: the distance between ownership and control is greater and it is more difficult to monitor the actions of managers when ownership is diffused. As far as expected costs of distress are concerned, small companies show higher expected distress costs (Zingales 1995): they are more likely to fail and have poor access to capital markets and during periods of distress, they suffer more from a drop in sales.

The positive link is also justified by the use of size as a proxy for other variables that have already been discussed. The size may have a negative link with leverage: if the company is large the magnitude of bankruptcy costs is greater (i.e., the bankruptcy procedure is longer and more complex), and because of the importance of implicit contracts, the recourse to debt may be discouraged. The larger size is often associated with greater diversification because it is linked to a greater dispersion of ownership: in manager-controlled companies, the diversification of non-systematic risk is carried out for managers at the firm level and not at the personal level.

Contrary to these hypotheses, the observed studies all find a negative link and some reasons for this result can be provided (Kim and Lyn 1991;

Opler and Titman 1993; Weir et al. 2005a; Leuz et al. 2008; Aslan and Kumar 2011; Martinez and Serve 2011).

Smaller companies incur greater information asymmetry: they are more difficult for investors to assess and there is less information transparency and financial visibility. For smaller companies, the costs of adverse selection (undervaluation of stocks) are higher. When information asymmetry increases, companies tend to leave the market (Leland and Pyle 1977; Chemmanur and Fulghieri 1999).

Large companies are more capable of bearing compliance costs and remaining in the market.

The entry into force of SOX in 2002 has often been cited as one of the main drivers of delisting in the US. Hostak et al. (2013), for example, point out that 77% of foreign companies that canceled themselves from the US markets, declared that they did so because of the high costs of complying with stock market regulation and over 40% of these companies referred directly to SOX. Chaplinsky and Ramchand (2012) and Bessler et al. (2012) suggest that SOX had a strong negative influence on the benefits of listing in the US. It is interesting to note that the implementation of SOX in the US triggered best practices in terms of corporate governance in Europe, reducing the probability of bankruptcy and liquidation (Thomsen and Vinten 2014). In 2005, the International Financial Reporting Standards (IFRS) were adopted in Europe. Listed companies in the EU, with consolidated financial statements, must apply these international standards which are also expensive. Vulcheva (2011) has shown that, like SOX, IFRS has also increased the propensity to delisting.

The impact of SOX on deregistration was studied with other determinants by Leuz et al. (2008): small businesses with low performance and growth opportunities, for which compliance costs are particularly heavy, are more likely to go dark.

3.3.6 Previous Performance

All statistically significant results show a negative relationship between performance and delisting (Opler and Titman 1993; Weir et al. 2005b; Weir and Wright 2006; Leuz et al. 2008; Weir et al. 2008; Aslan and Kumar 2011; Martinez and Serve 2011).

The result is consistent with the perspective of agency problems, information asymmetries and compliance costs. If delisted companies show poor performance, this choice could indicate high agency costs

(Weir et al. 2008) and value losses due to suboptimal investments. From the point of view of information asymmetries, the problem of adverse selection leads to a stock price that is lower than the real value. The undervaluation is an incentive to delisting. In addition, companies that show poorer performance suffer more from complying with stock exchange regulations.

On the other hand, for the positive link which has not been found empirically, Kashefi Pour and Lasfer (2013) hypothesize that companies that perform well (and have a high ROA) are more inclined to delist: if liquidity increases due to good performance, managerial discretion has to be limited (FCF hypothesis). In another sense, for companies that have already had disappointing stock market performance, the risks of incurring bankruptcy costs are greater and the fact that they prefer to exit the public market is excluded.

3.3.7 Company Age

Theories on takeovers state that young companies tend to be more subject to acquisitions, have greater financial constraints, and seek financial synergies with other companies. At the same time, they are more difficult to evaluate because they do not have enough historical information; in this case, listing may be preferred to the status of privately held firm in order to facilitate the trading of shareholdings on better conditions, given that the public market is more competitive than the private one (Zingales 1995). These aspects would justify a positive link between the company's age and the delisting. The lack of an adequate evaluation horizon could imply that less mature companies suffer the costs of adverse selection more. If this factor prevails over the need for trading, the link between company age and delisting could be negative.

Weir et al. (2008) believe that companies with less than 3 years since their IPO have greater distress risks. In this sense, older companies, which are quoted for longer, have lower expected costs of bankruptcy, and are more likely to opt for delisting (positive link).

All the studies that consider this determinant (Aslan and Kumar 2011; Opler and Titman 1993; Weir et al. 2008) find a negative and significant link, thereby confirming the hypothesis of asymmetric information problems and adverse selection costs.

3.3.8 *Taxation*

The tax determinant, measurable as a tax rate or the incidence of taxes paid in relation to other variables, can influence, with a positive link, the going private decision because taxes influence capital structure choices. The trade-off model (Myers 1984) theorizes that companies paying a high amount of taxes tend to prefer higher leverage, which can be achieved through LBOs, in order to take advantage of interest deductibility. The empirical evidence on the sign of the link is not univocal and some studies (Achleitner et al. 2013; Engel et al. 2007; Weir et al. 2005b, 2008) show a positive link; Achleitner et al. (2013) and Mehran and Peristiani (2010) show a negative link, but it is only significant for the latter study.

3.3.9 *Corporate Governance Quality*

With reference to the agency theory (Jensen and Meckling 1976), as has already emerged for other determinants, a significant part of the literature believes that the problem of realigning interests between managers and shareholders explains going private decisions. For companies with a diffused ownership structure, the separation between ownership and control generates conflicts of interests between managers and shareholders. This conflict of interests is an incentive to pursue private benefits when managers have a limited stake in the company.

These problems are more severe if the company suffers from inefficiencies in corporate governance and can be mitigated by GPTs (negative link between governance quality and GPTs).

The most commonly used governance variables are those able to account for the level of internal/external monitoring of the board's decisions: a low quality of governance due to a low level of monitoring, encourages cancelation. Boards with a large portion of independent directors are considered more monitored. Similarly, the board is considered more efficient if the CEO is not also the chairman of the board of directors (CEO duality); moreover, smaller boards suffer less from free riding problems than larger ones.

The sign of the link between the proxies and the delisting supports this position and companies with weaker governance (larger board size, lower percentage of independent directors, CEO duality) are more subject to delisting. However, the results are not always significant. Observing the significant ones, for the UK, Weir et al. (2005a, b),

Weir and Wright (2006) and Leuz et al. (2008) show that delisted companies are more likely to have a CEO who coincides with the chairman than those that remain listed. Leuz et al. (2008) find that companies with fewer independent directors are more likely to delist. This result may mean that stronger boards are more likely to prevent a company delisting if it is not in the shareholders' interests.

3.3.10 The Presence of Institutional Investors

In terms of governance quality and monitoring ability, some studies consider the fundamental role of institutional shareholders. Private equity investors can play a role in monitoring because they often require their own representatives to be on the board. These additional directors generally have important managerial skills that help the CEO in capital budgeting. Obviously, if there is more monitoring by an institutional investor, delisting is less necessary; on the other hand, if fewer institutional investors are present, the likelihood of cancelation from the stock market is greater.

The same link can be assumed considering that the costs of adverse selection, which arise in a context of asymmetric information, are lower if the presence of institutional investors is greater, since this improves the financial visibility of the company. Information asymmetry is greater if financial visibility is reduced. Financial visibility means the ability of an enterprise to attract an appropriate level of interest from investors.

This negative link is confirmed both in going private transactions (Bharath and Dittmar 2010; Mehran and Peristiani 2010) and in going dark operations (Leuz et al. 2008). In the case of LBOs, the determinant is also studied by Weir et al. (2005a, b) and Weir and Wright (2006): in contrast with other studies, they find that the presence of institutional investors is greater for delisted companies than for others.

3.3.11 Analyst Coverage

Mehran and Peristiani (2010) consider financial visibility and the interest of investors to be factors that are crucial to delisting decisions. Companies with less financial visibility tend to have high volatility of returns, fewer published recommendations, and lower trading volumes. They suffer more from information asymmetries and are therefore more likely to delist. The results by Martinez and Serve (2011) also confirm these hypotheses.

3.3.12 Insider Ownership and Ownership Concentration

If a manager holds a stake in the company he manages, the problem of interest realignment is lower when the percentage of his ownership is higher (negative link). However, the manager may decide to delist the firm to protect his controlling stake (positive link). Some companies that proceed with delisting have greater equity participation by the CEO, compared with companies that remain public, for another reason too. If the CEO is aware of profitable growth opportunities for the company that are however ignored by the market, it will be in his interest to maximize the value and proceed with delisting (Weir et al. 2005a; Leuz et al. 2008).

The ownership structure of European companies is traditionally concentrated with significant participation of the founding family. According to Achleitner et al. (2013), a high pre-delisting ownership concentration increases the probability of delisting in Europe and therefore the assumptions regarding the realignment of interests are not as strong in Europe as they are in the UK or US.

Weir et al. (2005a) show that a high ownership concentration implies fewer conflicts of interest between shareholders and managers, but these turn into conflicts between majority and minority shareholders when the former obtain private benefits of control to the detriment of the latter. These conflicts of interest are high if the majority shareholders behave in a way that pushes toward the exclusion of the minority ones. In this direction, Croci and Del Giudice (2014) believe that delisting could play a role in expropriating value from minority shareholders for at least two reasons. The first is that the majority shareholder could act on private information and delist the company before a performance improvement to avoid having to share this improvement with other shareholders. The second is that the majority shareholder is in a strong contractual position compared with the minority shareholder and does not need to pay a premium for control. For these reasons, the buyout price offered to minority shareholders is low. However, the empirical results do not seem to fully confirm these hypotheses.

The agency costs of debt are higher in companies in which managers hold a large portion of equity and are more incentivized to expropriate wealth from creditors in favor of shareholders (Jensen and Meckling 1976). For these companies it is more difficult to contract new debt, and GPTs are therefore less likely.

All the studies that observe a significant link between insider ownership and delisting (Aslan and Kumar 2011; Engel et al. 2007; Kashefi Pour and

Lasfer 2013; Weir et al. 2005a, b; Wright et al. 2006) identify a positive sign, confirming the assumptions on the protection of control and information asymmetries. Achleitner et al. (2013) make a distinction between different types of majority shareholders and argue that if the majority shareholder is a family, the risk of an excessive consumption of private benefits is greater, thus justifying a negative expected sign. Martinez and Serve (2011) in France show that the reasons for delisting via BOSO linked to corporate control may vary according to the type of shareholding. The family shareholders, in particular, aim to maximize their benefits, which often include private benefits that are not available to minority investors. In addition, families are often risk averse and will choose to exit the stock market when faced with threats to their control, this being truer for smaller and underestimated firms. Therefore, when the company is a family firm, the tendency to protect itself by leaving the market may be stronger.

3.3.13 *Speculation*

Quotation can serve as a first step toward a process of acquisition of the company because it makes it more visible with more attractive prices (Zingales 1995). These considerations suggest that firms that are not active in the market for corporate control tend to go private. No study among those examined finds a significant positive link.

3.3.14 *External Financial Needs*

The level of external financing needs is crucial. For example, companies that pay dividends or have greater investments in fixed assets generally have higher financing needs and are less likely to delist. The need to resort to external financing is reduced if the company does not have strong growth opportunities or capital expenditures to finance. The expected link between the capital expenditure/assets ratio and the probability of delisting is negative. These hypotheses are confirmed by Bharath and Dittmar (2010) and Kashefi Pour and Lasfer (2013).

3.3.15 *Liquidity*

Zingales (1995) highlights the importance of listing to establish the right price/market value and thus guarantee companies a source of liquidity for their stock. Liquidity has always been considered a benefit of listing, but if it deteriorates, firms tend to prefer to leave the public market. Companies are more inclined to exit the market when the market activity is less intense and the lack of negotiation leads to the determination of prices that do not always reflect the value of the underlying corporate assets and limits access to financial resources.

The results found by Leuz et al. (2008), Bharath and Dittmar (2010), Martinez and Serve (2011) and Achleitner et al. (2013) who find a negative link between trading volumes and the going private decision are in line with this position.

3.4 Reasons for Involuntary Delisting

The literature on involuntary delisting (Table 3.3) can be divided into two sub-strands.

A first group of studies argues that companies proceed to involuntary delisting because their performance makes it difficult for them to stay on the market. A second group of studies, on the other hand, argues that delisting can be explained either by insufficient regulation that protects market investors or by violation of the minimum requirements required by the stock exchange.

3.4.1 Performance

Almost all the studies in this strand focus on cancelation from the stock exchange of newly listed companies.

Seguin and Smoller (1997) examine two determinants of the mortality of new companies listed on the NASDAQ: the death rate is higher if the price and market capitalization are lower. Baker and Kennedy (2002) find high mortality for companies listed on the NYSE and AMEX (about 40% in 10 years) and study how much this depends on the stock returns before delisting. These companies lose a significant fraction of their value during the 10 years prior to cancelation. Other studies examine the survival rates on the market. Fama and French (2004) show the importance of performance deterioration before delisting for companies that went public by means of an IPO. Wagner and Cockburn (2010) analyze the impact of undervaluation on the involuntary delisting of Internet and software companies that have completed an IPO on the NASDAQ. The authors examine the role of patents in delisting. The results confirm their hypothesis: companies with few patents show weak performance and a high risk of involuntary delisting compared to those with more patents.

Table 3.3 The reasons for involuntary delisting

	Empirical study		
Determinant/hypothesis	**Proxies**	**Study**	**Link with delisting**[a]
Performance – The death rate is higher if the company: – performs less well and/or has low capitalization and/or a low market value in the previous period; – is less innovative; – has a poorer performance before and at the time of the IPO; – has low quality investors	Market capitalization (*t*)- market capitalization (*t*-10) when *t*=year of delisting	Seguin and Smoller (1997)	–
		Baker and Kennedy (2002)	–
	log(price) prior to delisting	Seguin and Smoller (1997)	–
	log (number of shares) prior to delisting	Seguin and Smoller (1997)	+
	EBITDA/total assets prior to delisting	Fama and French (2004)	–
	Number of patents prior to delisting	Wagner and Cockburn (2010)	–
	Firm's age when going public	Wagner and Cockburn (2010)	+
	ln (market value) at listing	Gerakos et al. (2013)	–
	Market to book value at listing	Gerakos et al. (2013)	–
	Capitalization/total assets prior to IPO	Peristiani and Hong (2004)	–
	ROA prior to IPO	Peristiani and Hong (2004)	–
	Earnings management (function of LogMV, LogShare, EBIT, leverage, Growth, VC presence) at listing	Li and Zhou (2006)	+
	log(number of shares) at listing	Li and Zhou (2006)	–
	% shareholding of venture capitalists	Bhattacharya et al. (2015)	–
	% shareholding of high quality investors	Bhattacharya et al. (2015)	–
	Abnormal returns prior to delisting	Sanger and Peterson (1990)	–

Regulation and Violation of Minimum Requirements – The death rate is greater if the regulation is less protective towards investors and companies tend to have difficulty in meeting the minimum requirements	Introduction of TUF	Cattaneo et al. (2015)	–
	Change in average scaled weekly trading volume	Sanger and Peterson (1990)	–
	Change in relative bid-ask spread	Sanger and Peterson (1990)	–
	Value spread	Serrano (2013)	–
	Change in average scaled weekly trading volume	Harris et al. (2008)	–
	Number of quotes per day	Harris et al. (2008)	–
	Core violations (net tangible assets, capitalization, total assets, total revenue, market makers)	Chen and Schoderbek (1999)	–
		Harris et al. (2008)	–
	Non-core violations (free float, market value of free float, minimum bid price)	Harris et al. (2008)	–

[a](−) = greater value of the determinant, lower probability of delisting; (+) = greater value of the determinant, greater probability of delisting; the significant results are highlighted in gray

Several studies state that characteristics in terms of performance at the time of listing may affect a company's survival rate on the market. Gerakos et al. (2013) compares companies delisted from the LSE and NASDAQ with those of the AIM: he finds that AIM companies have a higher failure rate and a greater risk of involuntary delisting than LSE companies because they show poorer performance before cancelation, but also a lower value at the time of listing. Peristiani and Hong (2004) show that delisted companies performed less well (lower ROA) and had a low equity/assets ratio before the IPO compared with a control sample. Li and Zhou (2006) focus on the quality of IPO companies by examining the link between earnings management in IPO and the risk of delisting. They assume that earnings management is inversely correlated with the quality of the enterprise and that quality is inversely correlated with the risk of delisting. In light of these links, companies with aggressive earnings management are more likely to be delisted from the stock market.

3.4.2 *Regulation and Violation of Minimum Requirements*

Cattaneo et al. (2015) focus on the relationship between regulation and the survival of IPO companies in Italy from 1861 to 2011. This period contains two sub-periods. The first one (1974–1997) is distinct from the second one with reference to the introduction of the "Testo Unico della Finanza" (Italian Law on Markets and Finance, also called the "Draghi Law") that came into force to meet the need for greater investor protection. The survival of IPO firms is higher after the Draghi reform than before.

By studying the firms in the NYSE and AMEX, Sanger and Peterson (1990) show that most delisting occurs after a period of negative abnormal returns and that abnormal returns are more negative when minimum standards are not met; in fact, value losses are partly due to a reduction in liquidity. Harris et al. (2008) analyze the reasons for delisting in the NASDAQ. The degree of uncertainty over future enterprise value and breaches of corporate governance rules are important factors. Violation of the minimum level of tangible assets and net profits, among the fundamental requirements, and minimum selling price and market value, among the non-fundamental requirements, are considered less serious violations. The authors also point to the fact that most companies that delisted from the NASDAQ continued to trade on other platforms.

Given that delisting rules in US stock exchanges are stringent and very detailed (see also Sect. 1.3), we might expect delisting to immediately follow violation of the minimum requirements. In contrast, Macey et al. (2008) show that there is flexibility in control by the US supervisory officials and some companies continue to be negotiated for months after violating the rules. Chen and Schoderbek (1999) analyze the involuntary delisting processes in the AMEX. First, they note that 45.7% of companies in their sample did not violate accounting standards before delisting whereas 31% violated them on several occasions in the 5 years prior to delisting. In addition, only 21.7% of companies that violated the criteria were canceled during the year following the first violation. The authors argue that companies delist from the AMEX only when, in addition to the violation of market rules, they initiate bankruptcy procedures, the trading volume and stock returns have been reduced, and the investor sentiment declines.

Macey et al. (2008) refer to a "delisting dilemma". Deciding when is the right time to proceed with delisting seems to depend on the one hand, on the moment that the rules are violated and on the other, on the flexibility that is granted. Delisting occurs later than violation because the stock exchanges have profit goals and it is difficult to decide to cancel companies from the market. The quotation rules aim to ensure that profitable companies remain public. When trading becomes sporadic, stock market gains fall and its costs increase, especially monitoring costs. Furthermore, the non-cancelation of a firm may be more expensive than cancelation if its reputation deteriorates.

In short, stock exchanges are cautious and cannot base their cancelation decision only on violation of criteria. Delisting processes are complex and often very expensive and it is inevitable that a trade-off is made in order to minimize costs. Macey et al. (2008) add that the dilemma could be solved by transferring responsibility for delisting to a regulatory body or by sharing responsibility between the stock exchange and the SEC in the US. The Market Regulatory Service in Canada has adopted a set of common rules for all Canadian stock exchanges. The stock exchange is free to apply additional rules, but any violation of the basic rules leads to immediate cancelation. Serrano (2013) compares delisting rules between the NYSE (a self-regulated market) and the Toronto Stock Exchange (TSX) where a regulatory body defines delisting rules. He states that self-regulation of the NYSE increases conflicts of interest and, as a result, expenses are higher for investors of companies delisted from the NYSE than for investors of firms delisted from the TSX.

3.5 Effect of Delisting on Shareholders' Wealth

The economic and financial consequences of delisting vary according to the type of delisting.

Involuntary delisting is not the consequence of a choice; therefore, it is often accompanied by a destruction of firm value. It is normally induced by a reduction in the price of the company's shares and/or productivity and, in some cases, by the persistence of situations of financial distress. This means that involuntary delisting is bad news for the market which suffers a value loss. On the other hand, voluntary delisting is a decision taken by management and its economic consequences vary according to the strategies the managers want to pursue by taking this decision. In this case, the value creation will depend on the ability of the company to create synergies after the deal.

Value effect is generally examined in literature through event studies or the observation of the premium between the offer price and the pre-delisting market price. The average premium paid by the buyers to the pre-transaction shareholders should be an expression of the potential additional value that will be generated after the company goes private.

Angel et al. (2004) and Harris et al. (2008) note that the quality of stock deteriorates when delisting is linked to financial distress. The authors observe quoted spread, trading volumes, and the volatility of delisted securities: trading volumes lose two-thirds of their value, the spread triples from 12.1% to 33.6%, and volatility also triples. Sanger and Peterson (1990) also show that the value of the company is negatively influenced by the decision to delist from the NYSE or the AMEX. They note that share prices drop 8.5% on the day delisting is announced. This loss of value can be caused by a reduction in liquidity. Another explanation for the decline in the value of the company is the negative signal that is issued with the decision of the stock exchange regarding the quality of the company. From another point of view, Eisdorfer (2008) examines the effects of delisting on profitability by testing the momentum strategy. The author compares the momentum profits of delisting due to mergers or bankruptcy and finds that, on average, about 40% of momentum profits is generated by the delisting yields. This difference is due to the firm's characteristics before delisting: failed companies show negative price trends before delisting due to their poor performance and thus produce momentum profits after delisting.

In contrast, although involuntary delisting destroys shareholders' wealth, significant wealth creation is expected from a voluntary delisting (via an LBO or a freeze-out) since the cancelation from the public market allows the firm to save on the listing costs (compliance costs and agency costs). In the UK and the US, the CARs are positive (between 19% and 30%, depending on the days on which they are calculated) and the premium is between 40% and 57% (DeAngelo et al. 1984; Kaplan 1989a; Lehn and Poulsen 1989; Renneboog et al. 2007).

The geographical location of delisted companies appears to be a determinant of the size of the premium. Except for Boubaker et al. (2014), in the European GPTs, the premium is lower than that observed in the US and the UK. For example, Bajo et al. (2013) observe a premium of 18.98% and Sannajust (2010) finds that shareholders who sell their shares will earn a 34% premium in the US, 29% in the UK and 20% in Europe.

A similar difference is also found in event studies in terms of cumulative abnormal returns. Depending on the event window, CARs change between 13% and 38% in the US (Lehn and Poulsen 1989 on a window of −20/+20 find CARs equal to 20.5%; Kaplan 1989a on a window of −40/+60 equal to 26%). Cumulative abnormal returns are much lower in Europe: 18.7% in Geranio and Zanotti (2012), 10.19% in Croci and Del Giudice (2014) and 22.3% in Boubaker et al. (2014), all on a window of −30/+30 days. Sannajust (2010) reports the following CARs: 12.53% in Europe versus 14.93% in the UK and 34.08% in the US (window −20/+ 20).

The results of Marosi and Massoud (2007) and Leuz et al. (2008) are in contrast to these. They focus on two reasons for going dark; poor performance on the one hand and the possibility of obtaining private benefits on the other. For these two reasons, deregistration has a negative effect on shareholders' wealth. The cumulative abnormal return in the twenty days around the event for the first study is about −11% whereas for the second one, it stands at around −7%.

To summarize, involuntary delisting typically produces negative effects on value whereas voluntary delisting produces positive effects that, in any case, depend on the geographical location. Governance characteristics and the tax profile of an LBO can also justify these results.

With reference to the corporate governance, the weaker positive effect in Europe compared to the UK and the US is often explained by the characteristics of different legal and governance systems. Faccio and Lang (2002) show that the ownership structure of most European companies is concentrated with a majority shareholder (often a family) exercising strong control. Achleitner et al. (2013) note that the shareholding held by majority shareholders in LBO targets in Europe is double that of both the UK and the US.

Renneboog et al. (2007) argue that the presence of a strong concentration before delisting implies lower wealth creation in GPTs because the company incurs lower agency costs and the benefit of delisting is therefore lower. The authors argue that the larger the stake held by another company, the stronger this result becomes. Andres et al. (2007) confirm the importance of monitoring and believe that the pre-LBO quality of governance influences the ability to create wealth for shareholders in Europe: companies with weak monitoring by shareholders tend to observe higher abnormal returns.

Other studies have rejected the hypothesis of the monitoring role of shareholders. Croci and Del Giudice (2014) verify the impact of family control on shareholders' wealth and observe that market reaction is negatively linked to the degree of ownership concentration. Boubaker et al. (2014) analyze the role of large shareholders in detail by studying the effect of separation between ownership and control. They highlight that the wider the separation between ownership and control, the less wealth is created for shareholders. Furthermore, they find that the wealth created is lower for companies with a second large shareholder than for companies with only one major shareholder. This result is explained by the monitoring effect of the second largest shareholder. Bajo et al. (2013) believe that institutional investors play a role in explaining the value creation in Italian delisting via BOSO. They find a positive association between the wealth created for shareholders of delisted companies and the presence of a foreign institutional investor who is also independent and active in the ownership structure. Institutional investors seem to play a monitoring role on majority shareholders.

Geranio and Zanotti (2012) obtain conflicting results: they show that delisting sought by shareholders of family firms produces more wealth for shareholders, whereas the presence of institutional investors and the participation of companies have no significant impact. Using a sample of German firms delisted via BOSO, Croci and Del Giudice (2014) show that CARs are greater when delisting is carried out by a family shareholder or by German shareholders.

Considering tax motivations, Kaplan (1989b) highlights the importance of tax advantages as one of the main sources of wealth for shareholders of companies delisted through an LBO. The debt used to finance the LBO creates benefits for companies because interest payments are tax deductible. The tax shield increases liquidity and shareholder value both in

Table 3.4 The effect of delisting on shareholders' wealth

Hypothesis	*Empirical study*		
	Effect on value: sign	*Effect on value*[a]	*Study*
Voluntary delisting can have both a positive and a negative effect on performance	+	CARs (−30, +30) = 24.2%	Andres et al. (2007)
		Premium = 8.98%	Bajo et al. (2013)
		CARs (−30, +30) = 22.3%; premium = 36.27%	Boubaker et al. (2014)
		CARs (−30, +30) = 10.19%	Croci and Del Giudice (2014)
		CARs (−20, +20) = 29.74%; premium = 56.3%	DeAngelo et al. (1984)
		CARs (−30, +30) = 18.7%	Geranio and Zanotti (2012)
		CARs (−40, +60) = 26%; premium = 40%	Kaplan (1989a, b)
		CARs (−20, +20) = 20.5%; premium = 36.1%	Lehn and Poulsen (1989)
		CARs (−40, +40) = 19.28%; premium = 40%	Renneboog et al. (2007)
		Premium Europe = 20%, premium USA = 34.08%, premium UK = 29%; CARs (−20, +20) Europe = 12.53%, CARs (−20, +20) USA = 34.08%; CARs (−20, +20) UK = 14.93%	Sannajust (2010)
	−	CARs (−20, +20) = −7.6%	Leuz et al. (2008)
		CARs (0, +1) = −10.99%	Marosi and Massoud (2007)
Involuntary delisting has a negative effect on performance	−	CARs (−2, +2) = −17.79%	Angel et al. (2004)
		Negative momentum profits = 40%	Eisdorfer (2008)
		Quoted spread triples	Harris et al. (2008)
		AR (0) = −8.5%	Sanger and Peterson (1990)

[a]*AR* = Abnormal return on event day, *CARs* = Cumulative abnormal returns, premium = % difference between offer price and pre-delisting market price

the US (Kieschnick 1998; Halpern et al. 1999) and in Europe (Achleitner et al. 2013). However, as noted by Renneboog et al. (2007), the amount of tax benefits depends on the tax regime and the marginal tax rate applied to the company's income: the tax benefit of financing companies by debt rather than equity is greater in the US than in the UK (Table 3.4).

References

Achleitner, A. K., Betzer, A., Goergen, V., & Hinterramskogler, B. (2013). Private equity acquisitions of continental European firms: The impact of ownership and control on the likelihood of being taken private. *European Financial Management, 19*(1), 72–107.

Andres, C., Betzer, A., & Weir, C. (2007). Shareholder wealth gains through better corporate governance. The case of European LBO-transactions. *Financial Markets and Portfolio Management, 21*, 403–424.

Angel, J., Harris, J., Panchapagesan, V., & Werner, I. (2004). From pink slips to pink sheets: Market quality around delisting from NASDAQ. Working paper, Ohio State University, Charles A. Dice Center for Research in Financial Economics.

Aslan, H., & Kumar, P. (2011). Lemons or cherries? Growth opportunities and market temptations in going public and private. *Journal of Financial and Quantitative Analysis, 46*(2), 489–526.

Bajo, E., Barbi, M., Bigelli, M., & Hillier, D. (2013). The role of institutional investors in public-to-private transactions. *Journal of Banking and Finance, 37*(11), 4327–4336.

Baker, G. P., & Kennedy, R. E. (2002). Survivorship and the economic grim reaper. The Journal of Law. *Economics, and Organization, 18*(2), 324–361.

Bessler, W., Kaen, F., Kurmann, R., & Zimmermann, J. (2012). The listing and delisting of German firms on NYSE and NASDAQ: Were there any benefits? *Journal of International Financial Markets, Institutions & Money, 22*(2), 1024–1053.

Bharath, S. T., & Dittmar, A. K. (2010). Why do firms use private equity to opt out of public markets? *Review of Financial Studies, 23*(5), 1771–1818.

Bhattacharya, U., Borisov, A., & Yu, X. (2015). Firm mortality and Natal financial care. *Journal of Financial and Quantitative Analysis, 50*(1), 61–88.

Boubaker, S., Cellier, A., & Rouatbi, W. (2014). The sources of shareholder wealth gains from going private transactions: The role of controlling shareholders. *Journal of Banking and Finance, 43*, 226–246.

Cattaneo, M., Meoli, M., & Vismara, S. (2015). Financial regulation and IPOs: Evidence from the history of the Italian stock market. *Journal of Corporate Finance, 31*, 116–131.

Chaplinsky, S., & Ramchand, L. (2012). What drives delistings of foreign firms from US exchanges? *Journal of International Financial Markets, Institutions & Money, 22*, 1126–1148.

Chemmanur, T. J., & Fulghieri, P. (1999). A theory of the going-public decision. *Review of Financial Studies, 12*(2), 249–279.

Chen, K. C. W., & Schoderbek, M. P. (1999). The role of accounting information in security exchange delisting. *Journal of Accounting and Public Policy, 31*(1), 31–57.

Croci, E., & Del Giudice, A. (2014). Delistings, controlling shareholders and firm performance in Europe. *European Financial Management, 20*(2), 374–405.

DeAngelo, H., DeAngelo, A., & Rice, E. (1984). Going private: Minority freeze outs and stockholder wealth. *Journal of Law and Economics, 27*, 367–401.

Doidge, C., Karolyi, A., & Stulz, R. M. (2013). The U.S. left behind? Financial globalization and the rise of IPOs outside the U.S. *Journal of Financial Economics, 110*(3), 546–573.

Eisdorfer, A. (2008). Delisted firms and momentum profits. *Journal of Financial Markets, 11*(2), 160–179.

Engel, E., Hayes, R. M., & Wang, X. (2007). The Sarbanes–Oxley Act and firms' going-private decisions. *Journal of Accounting and Economics, 44*(1), 116–145.

Faccio, M., & Lang, L. (2002). The ultimate ownership of Western European corporations. *Journal of Financial Economics, 65*(3), 365–395.

Fama, E. F., & French, K. R. (2004). New lists: Fundamentals and survival rates. *Journal of Financial Economics, 73*(2), 229–269.

Gao, X., Ritter, J. R., & Zhongyan, Z. (2013). Where have all the IPOs gone? *Journal of Financial and Quantitative Analysis, 48*(6), 1663–1692.

Gerakos, J., Lang, M., & Maffett, M. (2013). Post-listing performance and private sector regulation: The experience of London's alternative investment market. *Journal of Accounting and Economics, 56*(2), 189–215.

Geranio, M., & Zanotti, G. (2012). Equity markets do not fit all: An analysis of public-to-private deals in Continental Europe. *European Financial Management, 18*(5), 867–895.

Grullon, G., Larkin, Y., & Michaely, R. (2015). The disappearance of public firms and the changing nature of U.S. Industries. Working paper. http://ssrn.com/abstract=2612047

Halpern, P., Kieschnick, R., & Rotenberg, W. (1999). On the heterogeneity of leveraged going private transactions. *The Review of Financial Studies, 12*(2), 281–309.

Harris, J. H., Panchapagesan, V., & Werner, I. M. (2008). Off but not gone: A study of Nasdaq delistings. Working paper, Fisher College of Business.

Hostak, P., Lys, T., & Yang, Y. G. (2013). An examination of the impact of the Sarbanes–Oxley Act on the attractiveness of U.S. capital markets for foreign firms. *Review of Accounting Studies, 18*(2), 522–559.

Jensen, M. C. (1986). Agency costs of free cash flow, corporate finance, and takeovers. *American Economic Review, 76*(2), 323–329.

Jensen, M. C. (1989). Eclipse of the public corporation. *Harvard Business Review, 67*(5), 61–37.

Jensen, M. C., & Meckling, H. (1976). Theory of the firm: Managerial behavior, agency costs and ownership structure. *Journal of Financial Economics, 3*(4), 305–350.

Kaplan, S. (1989a). The effects of management buyouts on operations and value. *Journal of Financial Economics, 24*(2), 217–254.

Kaplan, S. (1989b). Management buyouts: Evidence of taxes as a source of value. *Journal of Finance, 44*(3), 611–632.

Kashefi Pour, E., & Lasfer, M. (2013). Why do companies delist voluntarily from the stock market? *Journal of Banking and Finance, 37*(12), 4850–4860.
Kieschnick, R. L. (1998). Free cash-flow and stockholder gains in going private transactions revisited. *Journal of Business Finance and Accounting, 25*(1–2), 187–202.
Kim, W. S., & Lyn, E. O. (1991). Going private: Corporate restructuring under information asymmetry and agency problems. *Journal of Business Finance and Accounting, 18*(2), 637–648.
Kim, W., & Weisbach, M. S. (2008). Motivations for public equity offers: An international perspective. *Journal of Financial Economics, 87*(2), 281–307.
Lehn, K., & Poulsen, A. (1989). Free cash flow and stockholder gains in going private transactions. *Journal of Finance, 44*(3), 771–787.
Leland, H. E., & Pyle, D. H. (1977). Informational asymmetries, financial structure and financial intermediations. *Journal of Finance, 32*(2), 371–387.
Leuz, C. (2007). Was the Sarbanes–Oxley Act of 2002 really this costly? A discussion of evidence from event returns and going-private decisions. *Journal of Accounting and Economics, 44*(1–2), 140–165.
Leuz, C., Triantis, A., & Wang, T. Y. (2008). Why do firms go dark? Causes and economic consequences of voluntary SEC deregistrations. *Journal of Accounting & Economics, 45*, 181–208.
Li, J., & Zhou, J. (2006). Earning management and delisting risk of initial public offering. Working paper, Simon School, University of Rochester.
Macey, J., O'Hara, M., & Pompilio, D. (2008). Down and out in the stock market: The law and economics of the delisting process. *Journal of Law and Economics, 51*(4), 683–713.
Marosi, A., & Massoud, N. (2007). Why do firms go dark? *Journal of Financial and Quantitative Analysis, 42*(2), 421–442.
Martinez, I., & Serve, S. (2011). The delisting decision: The case of buyout offer with squeeze-out (BOSO). *International Review of Law and Economics, 31*(4), 229–239.
Martinez, I., & Serve, S. (2017). Reasons for delisting and consequences: A literature review and research agenda. *Journal of Economic Surveys, 31*(3), 733–770.
Mehran, H., & Peristiani, S. (2010). Financial visibility and the decision to go private. *Review of Financial Studies, 23*(2), 519–547.
Myers, S. (1977). Determinants of corporate borrowing. *Journal of Financial Economics, 5*, 147–175.
Myers, S. (1984). The capital structure puzzle. *Journal of Finance, 39*(3), 575–592.
Opler, T., & Titman, S. (1993). The determinants of leveraged buyout activity: Free cash flow vs. financial distress costs. *Journal of Finance, 48*(5), 1985–1999.
Peristiani, S., & Hong, G. (2004). Pre-IPO financial performance and aftermarket survival. *Current Issues in Economics and Finance, 10*(2), 1–8.
Renneboog, L., Simons, T., & Wright, M. (2007). Why do public firms go private in the UK? The impact of private equity investors, incentive realignment and undervaluation. *Journal of Corporate Finance, 13*(4), 591–628.

Sanger, G. C., & Peterson, J. D. (1990). An empirical analysis of common stock delisting. *Journal of Financial and Quantitative Analysis, 25*(2), 261–273.

Sannajust, A. (2010). Motivations and performance of public to private operations: An international study. *Journal of Modern Accounting and Auditing, 6*(9), 1–19.

Seguin, P. J., & Smoller, M. M. (1997). Share price and mortality: An empirical evaluation of newly listed Nasdaq stocks. *Journal of Financial Economics, 45*(3), 333–363.

Serrano, A. (2013). Two essays on regulation. Ph.D. dissertation, Graduate School – Newark Rutgers, The State University of New Jersey. doi:https://doi.org/10.7282/T3GM859S

Shleifer, A., & Vishny, R. W. (1992). Liquidation value an debt capacity: A market equilibrium approach. *Journal of Finance, 47*(4), 1343–1366.

Thomsen, S., & Vinten, F. (2014). Delistings and the costs of governance: A study of European stock exchanges 1996–2004. *Journal of Management and Governance, 18*(3), 793–833.

Titman, S., & Wessels, R. (1988). The determinants of capital structure choice. *Journal of Finance, 43*(1), 1–19.

Vulcheva, M. I. (2011). International accounting standardization across countries with unequal enforcement – Questionable benefits at a high price? Ph.D. dissertation, Faculty of the James T. Laney School Emory University.

Wagner, S., & Cockburn, I. (2010). Patents and the survival of internet-related IPOs. *Research Policy, 39*, 214–228.

Weir, C., & Wright, M. (2006). Governance and takeovers: Are public-to-private transactions different from traditional acquisitions of listed corporations? *Accounting and Business Research, 36*(4), 289–307.

Weir, C., Laing, D., & Wright, W. (2005a). Incentive effects, monitoring mechanisms and the market for corporate control: An analysis of the factors affecting public to private transactions in the UK. *Journal of Business Finance and Accounting, 32*(5), 909–943.

Weir, C., Laing, D., & Wright, M. (2005b). Undervaluation, private information, agency costs and the decision to go private. *Applied Financial Economics, 15*(3), 947–961.

Weir, C., Wright, M., & Scholes, L. (2008). Public-to-private buy-outs, distress costs and private equity. *Applied Financial Economics, 18*(10), 801–819.

Wright, M., Renneboog, L., Simons, T., & Scholes, L. (2006). Leveraged buyouts in the U.K. and Continental Europe: Retrospect and prospect. *Journal of Applied Corporate Finance, 18*(3), 38–55.

Zingales, L. (1995). Insider ownership and the decision to go public. *Review of Economic Studies, 62*(3), 425–448.

CHAPTER 4

Voluntary Delisting and Agency Costs: The Case of the London Stock Exchange

Alberto Pezzi

4.1 Introduction

Over the last 20 years, the phenomenon of delisting has become more significant than IPOs in terms of figures in US, UK, and the majority of Continental Europe stock exchanges (see Chap. 1 for data and figures). This behavior can be explained as a consequence of market conditions and the sentiment of investors which influence the management decision to go public during bull markets (2004–2007) or delist the company during bear stock markets (2001–2003 and 2008–2009). However, delisting still remains an issue that has received little attention compared with IPOs (Croci and Del Giudice 2014; Kashefi Pour and Lasfer 2013; Liu et al. 2012; Sanger and Peterson 1990; Belkhir et al. 2013).

In this chapter we consider delisting as the removal of a listed company from a stock exchange and analyze voluntary delisting where the firm decides to go private and is not forced to delist from the stock exchange for two main reasons: poor firm performance and/or a violation of stock exchange requirements (the so-called involuntary delisting).

Martinez and Serve (2017) observe a heterogeneity of reasons for voluntary delisting linked primarily to cost-benefit analysis. Direct costs of listing include, for example, registration and underwriting fees and trading costs while indirect costs include compliance costs (Leuz et al. 2008; Thomsen and Vinten 2014 found an increase in delisting after the

B. Fidanza et al., *The Decision to Delist from the Stock Market*,
https://doi.org/10.1007/978-3-319-95049-5_4

Sarbanes-Oxley Act was introduced in 2002) that are not borne by private firms. Firms voluntarily delist because they are unable to obtain listing benefits exceeding incurred costs. Managers may decide to go private when firms are unable to find external financing from the public market, rebalance their capital structure or attract an adequate level of investor interest and recognition (Mehran and Peristiani 2010).

Studying why firms exit public markets can provide new evidence on existing trade-offs between the costs and benefits of being public. Aslan and Kumar (2011) discuss if the decision to go public or private is a stock-market-driven "sideshow" or if it has significant effects on investment and profitability. Their results show that firms with high financing needs, lower information production costs, and high industry market-to-book ratios are more likely to go public. The reasons for delisting should be the "other way around". We assess whether firms decide to go private because they do not have market access and if this is due to agency problems or asymmetric information.

In this chapter, we study the drivers of voluntary delisting from the LSE main market and the impact of the delisting process on agency costs. Our sample includes 108 firms from different industries delisted from the LSE between 2010 and 2016. We build a control group of 781 firms, selecting those listed from the same industries and with total assets 1 year prior to delisting that do not differ by more than 30%. We use the OLS model to test our hypotheses and collect accounting and financial data from Thomson Reuters Datastream. In particular, we want to explain the level and variability of ROA and the ratio between free cash flow and total assets as a proxy of agency costs through leverage (LEV) and market-to-book ratio (MB) as proxies for market access, intangible assets on total assets (INTANGIB) as proxy for asymmetric information, and the company's listing age (YOUNG).

4.2 Literature Review

The voluntary nature of delisting is strictly dependent on the net benefits that determine the going private transaction. Cost savings are a primary incentive for delisting because the decision to go private allows the firm to eliminate those costs that are incurred by the listed firm. Bharath and Dittmar (2010), for example, find that firms without large investment plans, with low visibility, or difficulties in receiving external financing from the stock market should be more likely to go private. The going private decision is therefore motivated by the loss of those incentives that induced the firm to go public in the past. In our work, we try to analyze agency costs and their influence on delisting decisions and the characteristics of listed firms.

The LBO literature has found a strong relationship between delisting and implications of agency conflicts and information asymmetries between principals and agents. Agency problems between managers and shareholders are rigorously analyzed in large listed firms with low growth opportunities and high free cash flows (Jensen 1986).

Firms incur agency costs when free cash flows are used in negative net present value (NPV) projects instead of being distributed to shareholders. Therefore, firms with significant free cash flow and low growth opportunities are more likely to go private through LBOs because cash flows are bound for debt repayment, thereby reducing cash flows wasted by managers (Jensen 1986, 1989).

The empirical tests of the free cash flow hypothesis, using a fraction of undistributed cash flows as a proxy, provide mixed results. In the US, Lehn and Poulsen (1989), Opler and Titman (1993) and Leuz et al. (2008) find evidence that free cash flow is a significant factor affecting the delisting decision. In contrast, Aslan and Kumar (2011), Kieschnick (1998) and Halpern et al. (1999) find negative results on the free cash flow hypothesis.

Growth opportunities are an important factor in the free cash flow hypothesis; low growth firms are potentially less able to find positive NPV investments for their funds. Bharath and Dittmar (2010) and Aslan and Kumar (2011) find that firms with high growth opportunities prefer to remain in the market to raise further capital. Marosi and Massoud (2007) report that free cash flow is significant for firms with high undistributed cash flows and low growth opportunities and this result is consistent with the fact that the LBO is not the prevalent form of delisting in the US. It is also important to underline that a sort of delisting wave can influence the results of empirical studies. Bharath and Dittmar (2010) find that in the 1980s, firms with higher free cash flows were interested in delisting procedures, but after 1990, going private was not strictly dependent on reducing free cash flow problems.

In Europe, firms consider the need to finance growth opportunities to be a significant determinant of the going-public decision (Bancel and Mittoo 2009) but the free cash flow hypothesis is not confirmed (Weir et al. 2005; Renneboog et al. 2007; Andres et al. 2007; Geranio and Zanotti 2012; Kashefi Pour and Lasfer 2013).

The agency-cost hypothesis predicts that firms, after going private, will improve profitability, reduce assets and investments, and increase leverage. The decision to delist seems to be associated with ex-ante lower performance in terms of sales growth, return on assets, and operating margin compared to the control group of listed firms (Lehn and Poulsen 1989; Kashefi Pour and Lasfer 2013; Weir and Wright 2006; Thomsen and Vinten 2014).

Access to public markets enhances a firm's transparency and improves its ability to access external financing through diversified financing channels such as banks, public debt, public equity, and so on (Ritter 1987; Pagano et al. 1998; Bharath and Dittmar 2010). Pagano et al. (1998) find that some firms go public to rebalance their capital structure or finance their growth opportunities. Consequently, Aslan and Kumar (2011) find that leverage has a positive effect on the going-private decision. Firms that are not able to rebalance their debt ratio decide to go private (Bancel and Mittoo 2009) and firms that voluntarily delist from the public market usually exhibit higher leverage than control firms (Kashefi Pour and Lasfer 2013). They find that firms failed to raise additional capital during their period as listed firms. After going public, leverage and insider ownership stayed very high, they did not raise equity capital, and their profitability, growth opportunities, and trading volume declined substantially. In other words, they increase their risk of bankruptcy. In this case, going private decision may reveal a firm's preference for alternative sources of financing, such as debt, that have lower costs than staying listed (Martinez and Serve 2011).

The visibility and the ability to attract new investors help firms to share risk more efficiently because investors eliminate idiosyncratic risk by maintaining well-diversified portfolios (Shah and Thakor 1988). However, if the stock is undervalued according to the managers' expectations, a firm may prefer to go private and reduce listing costs. Several studies confirm that delisted firms are undervalued compared with their listed counterparts (Weir et al. 2005; Renneboog et al. 2007; Bharath and Dittmar 2010; Croci and Del Giudice 2014; Thomsen and Vinten 2014).

We therefore expect the delisting decision to be influenced by the fact that firms cannot raise equity capital to rebalance their capital structure and are not able to become more visible and fairly valued by the market. We use different variables to measure leverage, growth opportunities, and stock undervaluation and we expect delisted firms to be characterized by low growth, high leverage, and a low probability of raising equity capital.

Several studies analyze the role asymmetric information plays on a firm's decision to go private. Small firms face difficulties attracting investors and investor recognition and when their financial visibility deteriorates or does not increase after the listing, they prefer to go back to being private (Mehran and Peristiani 2010). The firm size hypothesis was successfully tested and there is empirical evidence that large firms are potentially more efficient at amortizing listing costs than small firms (Kim and Lyn 1991; Kieschnick 1998; Engel et al. 2007; Weir et al. 2005; Bartlett 2009).

A lack of visibility can increase adverse selection problems and the probability of delisting of firms with asymmetric information (Bharath and Dittmar 2010). One of the most commonly used proxies for measuring adverse selection problems is the proportion of intangible assets over total assets (Kashefi Pour and Lasfer 2013; Pagano et al. 1998; Bharath and Dittmar 2010). We therefore suppose that small firms with high intangible assets are more likely to go private.

Although the main focus of this chapter is to analyze agency costs, there are other explanations proposed by the literature that can justify the decision to opt out of the public market. Bharath and Dittmar (2010) employ a comprehensive sample of going private transactions from 1980 to 2004 in the US and examine how these firms differ over their public life (from IPO to going private) compared with a sample of firms that went and remained public. They apply a Difference-in-Difference approach and use the sector and firm's age at the time of going private as matching variables. Young firms in terms of listing decide to go private because they have failed to reach an adequate level of visibility and investor recognition. Young firms are often overlooked by financial analysts and do not completely understand the costs and benefits of a public listing (Krigman et al. 2001).

Kashefi Pour and Lasfer (2013) analyze the motives and market valuation of voluntary delisting from the London AIM. These results hold even after controlling for agency, asymmetric information, and liquidity effects, and suggest that firms voluntarily delist when they fail to benefit from listing; they apply a logit model and create a control group composed of firms of a similar size with the same IPO date as the delisted ones, without controlling for the sector.

Lehn and Poulsen (1989) investigate the source of stockholder gains in going private transactions. They find support for the hypothesis that a major source of these gains is the mitigation of agency problems. Delisting sample includes 263 successful going private transactions from 1980 through 1987, collected by The Wall Street Journal Index; they create a control group matching firms with the same four-digit SIC code whose market value of equity most closely matched the sample, 1 year before the going-private transaction.

Croci and Del Giudice (2014) investigate the role of controlling shareholders in delisting decisions by relying on a sample of European firms. OLS model is used to evaluate the factors explaining the announcement effect on stock returns; they show that minority shareholders earn lower abnormal returns when the controlling shareholder takes the company private, but this lower premium disappears when they control for the firm's characteristics. After delisting, firms delisted by their controlling shareholders do not improve their operating performance. These results do not suggest that controlling shareholders expropriate minority investors by means of minority freeze-outs.

Studies that focus on particular groups of firms or markets have produced different results. For example, Boers et al. (2017) study the process of going private in family firms by applying a socioemotional wealth perspective. They propose that the experiences from being listed can lead to the revaluation of financial, as well as socioemotional wealth considerations. By means of delisting, a company reclaims independence and control and its identity as a private family-owned firm becomes once again pronounced. Du et al. (2013) examine a sample of going-private transactions in the Hong Kong stock market from 1989 to 2008. They find that privatized firms experience large negative abnormal returns prior to the announcement of going-private transactions, particularly in those firms with a weak corporate governance structure and a high level of related party transactions. The likelihood of going private is high in those poorly governed firms with large free cash flow. Unlike Croci and Del Giudice (2014), Du et al. (2013) conclusions suggest that controlling shareholders carry out self-dealings that lead to value losses and depressed stock prices.

Finally, Belkhir et al. (2013) confirm results by analyzing the specific case of France. They construct a sample of 161 firms that went private between 1997 and 2009 with a propensity-score-matched sample of firms that remained public during the same period. The results indicate that unlike firms that remained public, the largest controlling shareholders (LCSs) of firms going private controlled their firms by using an incommensurately small fraction of ultimate cash flow rights. This is consistent with the view that agency problems between large and minority shareholders make public firms less attractive to investors which reduces the benefits of staying public and encourages the LCSs to take their firms private or accept takeover offers. Additional results show that going private firms have more undervalued stocks and higher free cash flows than firms not going private. Expected interest tax shields, low growth opportunities, and pre-going-private takeover interest do not seem to affect the probability of delisting.

4.3 Data and Methodology

The sample includes all non-financial firms who voluntarily delisted from the London Stock Exchange's main market between 2010 and 2016. We hand collected the delisting year, company name, IPO date, and industry code from the LSE website. The sample initially included 225 firms and for each one we collected the RIC code required to download accounting and financial data from Thomson Reuters Datastream. The number dropped to 140 after controlling whether firms returned listed after a few years or whether the exclusion from the market was due to mergers or acquisitions. We then built the control group selecting all companies listed on the LSE within the same industry (GICS code) and with total assets in the year before delisting that do not differ by more than 30%. The control group includes more than 1000 observations. Variables are observed 1 year before delisting to mitigate a possible endogenous effect. Table 4.1 shows the definition of variables and the source of data.

Because the Durbin-Watson test indicates the presence of autocorrelation, we redesigned the database by inserting one observation for each company, calculated as the average of observations from 2010 to 2016 (Table 4.2 shows descriptive statistics).

Table 4.1 Variable definitions

Symbol	*Name*	*Description*	*Sources*
delist	Delist dummy	A dummy variable taking value 1 if the firm is delisted, 0 otherwise	LSE website
LEV	Leverage	Total debt/total assets	Datastream
MB	Market-to-book ratio	Market value over book value of equity	Datastream
ROA	Return on assets	Net income/total assets	Datastream
INTANGIB	Intangible	Intangible assets/total assets	Datastream
YOUNG		Difference between IPO date and delisting date (for delisted firms) and difference between IPO date and 2017 (for listed firms)	
FCFTA	Free cash flow	Free cash flow/total assets	Eikon
agency costs		Combination of ROA and FCFTA through PCA	Boardman et al. (1997)
TA (million)	Total assets	Total assets	Datastream

Table 4.2 Descriptive statistics

	N	*Minimum*	*Maximum*	*Mean*	*Std. deviation*
LEV	1187	0.004	43171.018	68.975	1267.932
MB	1147	−126.345	266.535	3.203	14.938
YOUNG	1187	0	85	13.82	12.846
ln_intangib	1137	−11.51	−0.03	−1.914	1.557
agency costs	1184	−6901.705	1763.578	−91.208	351.599

Table 4.3 Number of delistings

Year	2010	2011	2012	2013	2014	2015	2016	Total
Delist n.	25	12	17	15	23	29	19	140

Table 4.3 shows the distribution of the number of delistings over time.

The proposed analysis wants to investigate the relationship between agency costs and a firm's delisting process. Listed companies potentially suffer from agency conflict between managers and shareholders (Jensen 1986) and this risk increases with the firm's listing age (YOUNG). Furthermore, empirical studies provide mixed results on the role of free cash flow (FCFTA) in going-private decisions (Marosi and Massoud 2007; Lehn and Poulsen 1989); for these reasons we also control for agency conflicts measured by ROA which could cause endogeneity in the model. We include independent variables which are widely used as proxies for limited market access: leverage (LEV) and market-to-book ratio (MB). Finally, we also include intangible assets to total assets ratio (INTANGIB) to control for asymmetric information that tends to influence the delisting decision (Mehran and Peristiani 2010; Bharath and Dittmar 2010).

We want to explain whether there is a systematic relationship between agency costs and delisting choices and how delisting decisions can affect the increase or decrease in agency costs. Specifically, we want to calculate if the delisting process involves companies with different financial and business characteristics.

The methodological approach relies on OLS regressions through SPSS software. The identification of the dependent variable is based on the combination of two variables, ROA and the ratio between free cash flow and total assets (FCFTA), through a principal components analysis (PCA) and exploratory factor analysis (EFA).

Table 4.4 Correlations between independent variables

		Correlation				
		LEV	*MB*	*delist*	*YOUNG*	*ln_intangib*
LEV	Pearson correlation	1	−0.009	−0.012	−0.013	0.008
	Sig. (2-tailed)		0.753	0.69	0.656	0.775
	N	1187	1147	1187	1187	1137
MB	Pearson correlation	−0.009	1	−0.011	−0.029	−0.017
	Sig. (2-tailed)	0.753		0.702	0.328	0.562
	N	1147	1147	1147	1147	1102
delist	Pearson correlation	−0.012	−0.011	1	0.108**	−0.05
	Sig. (2-tailed)	0.69	0.702		0	0.089
	N	1187	1147	1187	1187	1137
YOUNG	Pearson correlation	−0.013	−0.029	0.108**	1	−0.015
	Sig. (2-tailed)	0.656	0.328	0		0.62
	N	1187	1147	1187	1187	1137
ln_intangib	Pearson correlation	0.008	−0.017	−0.05	−0.015	1
	Sig. (2-tailed)	0.775	0.562	0.089	0.62	
	N	1137	1102	1137	1137	1137

**Correlation is significant at the 0.01 level (2-tailed)

This process is justified because of the high correlation between ROA and FCFTA (0.811**). According to Boardman et al. (1997), we combine these two variables and rename the resulting variable as "agency costs".

We also calculate the correlations between all the independent variables in Table 4.4.

The model we test is as follows:

$$\text{agency costs}_{i,t} = \alpha + \beta_1 \text{LEV}_i + \beta_2 \text{MB}_i + \beta_3 \ln\_\text{intangib}_i + \beta_4 \text{YOUNG}_i + \beta_5 \text{delist}_{(0;1)} + \varepsilon_i \quad (4.1)$$

We want to investigate whether agency costs are a function, among other variables, of delisting choices. Indeed, a predominant reason for this type of choice is linked to a reduction in agency costs which are particularly burdensome in companies with fragmented ownership and seeking restructuring in order to face growing global market competition and the shocks induced by technological innovation. This motivation, supported by Jensen (1986, 1989) and widely reflected in empirical literature, falls within the agency theory for which the market effects acquisitions of the entire share capital (buyout), correcting corporate governance inefficiencies, mainly caused by the misalignment of interests between management and shareholders.

4.4 Results

In order to estimate the effect of the dummy variable (delist) on agency costs, we estimate a first regression model which only includes the constant and the dummy variable (Table 4.5).

From the output we obtain the following expression for the estimated model:

$$\text{agency costs}_{i,t} = \alpha + \beta_1 \text{delist}_{(0;1)} + \varepsilon_i \tag{4.2}$$

For delist = 1 (firms no longer listed on the stock exchange) (Eq. 4.3) and for delist = 0 (firms still listed on the stock exchange) (Eq. 4.4):

$$\text{agency costs}_{i,t} = -101.315 + 85.470_{\text{delist}(1)} \tag{4.3}$$

$$\text{agency costs}_{i,t} = -101.315 \tag{4.4}$$

These results show that, all other things being equal, agency costs increase by 85.470 US dollars for firms that have decided to undertake the delisting process.

Indeed, there are many studies in literature that describe the delisting process as a negative process for the company. Chandy et al. (2004) tend to bring out the negative nature of delisting since the company gives up the benefits associated with the status as a listed firm, shareholders see the

Table 4.5 Regression model between agency costs and delisting

Model	*Unstandardized coefficients*		*Standardized coefficients*	*t*	*Sign.*
	B	*Standard error*	*Beta*		
(Constant)	−101.315	10.853		−9.335	0.000
delist	85.470	31.561	0.079	2.708	0.007

Dependent variable: agency costs

value and liquidity of their securities to fall, managers lose prestige and visibility, and the stock exchange suffers worsening the IPO-delisting differential, losing attractiveness, prestige, and the benefits of the quotation and negotiation fees paid in advance by the delisted company.

We now estimate the model (Eq. 4.1) by considering the other independent variables in order to understand if the model improves its significance and in what way the corporate and financial variables influence the agency costs.

We present the results of the model (Eq. 4.1) in Tables 4.6 and 4.7.

First of all, the model's R^2 is 0.06, which does not represent a high value, but one that is still satisfactory given the nature of the data. The autocorrelation diagnostics show no problem in the model (Durbin-Watson = 1.990).

Table 4.6 indicates that the F test is equal to 13.942; the p-value is lower than the threshold of 0.05; we therefore reject the null hypothesis according to which all the parameters are not significant and conclude that the model, in its entirety, is significant.

Furthermore, the results show that there is no multicollinearity in the sample because the variance inflation factor (VIF) and tolerance index are far from the critical thresholds. Table 4.7 shows that leverage, delist, and YOUNG variables are significant ($t=-6.203$ and $p = 0.00$ for "Leverage"; $t = 2.843$ and $p = 0.005$ for "delist"; $t = 4.039$ and $p = 0.00$ for "Young") while market-to-book ratio and ln_intangib are not.

Macey et al. (2008) add that the first impact of the delisting announcement is on share price which decreases considerably. Their data show that the process of delisting is often long and expensive due to unclear regulations.

In addition, it is important to highlight that the coefficient of the leverage variable is negative, highlighting that the increase in leverage is associated with a decrease in agency costs.

Table 4.6 ANOVA regression model

Model		*Sum of square*	*gf*	*Mean square*	*F*	*Sign.*
1	Regression	5,860,492.854	5	1,172,098.571	13.942	0.000[a]
	Residual	91,886,976.634	1093	84,068.597		
	Total	97,747,469.488	1098			

Dependent variable: delist

[a]Predictors: (constant), agency costs, MB, LEV, YOUNG, INTANGIB

Table 4.7 Regression model

Model	*Unstandardized coefficients*		*Standardized coefficients*	*t*	*Sign.*	*Collinearity statistics*	
	B	*Standard error*	*Beta*			*Tolerance*	*VIF*
(Constant)	−112.345	17.095		−6.571	0.000		
LEV	−0.273	0.044	−0.182	−6.203	0.000	0.998	1.002
MB	0.525	0.575	0.027	0.913	0.362	0.999	1.001
ln_intangib	9.084	5.694	0.047	1.595	0.111	0.996	1.004
YOUNG	2.753	0.682	0.119	4.039	0.000	0.989	1.011
delist	75.737	26.636	0.084	2.843	0.005	0.988	1.012

Dependent variable: agency costs

4.5 Conclusions

In this chapter we have tried to frame the phenomenon of delisting, highlighting its multiform nature and the various aspects that characterize it. Its recent diffusion and limited doctrinal contributions, above all in the European context, mean that it still exhibits unclear aspects. Hence, interest lies in carrying out an accurate cross-sectional analysis with the aim of favoring a better understanding and investigating the main economic, financial, and cultural aspects related to the delisting phenomenon.

First, the phenomenon of delisting has been analyzed by focusing on the characteristics of the firms and relating it to the variation of agency costs, with the intention of drawing some interesting conclusions regarding the recurrence of the operation, the motivations and techniques, the years spent on the stock market by delisted firms, and the most affected sectors.

We highlight how agency costs are linked both to delisting processes and to other firm variables such as leverage or the number of years that a firm remains listed on the stock exchange.

This shows that delisting is an operation that has both positive and negative consequences and must therefore be analyzed and carefully weighed by the stock exchange. It is also important to bear in mind that not all low-quality firms, that is, companies with poor economic and financial performance, should be excluded from the quotation, but the possibility of recovery which provides support to avoid delisting should be considered.

Some factors are important for the process and delisting choices, including a significant analyst coverage that indicates the investor recognition for which the company is able to guarantee an important trading volume for its shares, favoring a positive trend in terms of price and liquidity. Furthermore, another factor that justifies this firm's process is the state of health at the time of the IPO and its size, in terms of equity and assets. Therefore, firms that have good fundamentals, in particular appreciable levels of earnings, ROA, turnover, and debt have more chances of staying on the regulated market for a longer period.

When one or more of these factors fail, there is a possibility that the company will delist from the stock market which will deprive it of the benefits linked to the listing but will also give greater freedom in terms of disclosure and a reduction in listing costs.

References

Andres, C., Betzer, A., & Weir, C. (2007). Shareholder wealth gains through better corporate governance—The case of European LBO-transactions. *Financial Markets and Portfolio Management, 21*(4), 403–424.

Aslan, H., & Kumar, P. (2011). Lemons or cherries? Growth opportunities and market temptations in going public and private. *Journal of Financial and Quantitative Analysis, 46*(2), 489–526.

Bancel, F., & Mittoo, U. R. (2009). Why do European firms go public? *European Financial Management, 15*(4), 844–884.

Bartlett, R. (2009). Going private but staying public: Reexamining the effect of Sarbanes-Oxley on firms' going-private decisions. *The University of Chicago Law Review, 76*(1), 7–44.

Belkhir, M., Boubaker, S., & Rouatbi, W. (2013). Excess control, agency costs and the probability of going private in France. *Global Finance Journal, 24*(3), 250–265.

Bharath, S. T., & Dittmar, A. K. (2010). Why do firms use private equity to opt out of public markets? *Review of Financial Studies, 23*, 1771–1818.

Boardman, A. E., Shapiro, D. M., & Vining, A. R. (1997). The role of agency costs in explaining the superior performance of foreign MNE subsidiaries. *International Business Review, 6*(3), 295–317.

Boers, B., Ljungkvist, T., Brunninge, O., & Nordqvist, M. (2017). Going private: A socioemotional wealth perspective on why family controlled companies decide to leave the stock-exchange. *Journal of Family Business Strategy, 8*(2), 74–86.

Chandy, P. R., Sarkar, S. K., & Tripathy, N. (2004). Empirical evidence on the effects of delisting from the national market system. *Journal of Economics and Finance, 28*(1), 46–55.

Croci, E., & Del Giudice, A. (2014). Delistings, controlling shareholders and firm performance in Europe. *European Financial Management, 20*(2), 374–405.

Du, J., He, Q., & Yuen, S. W. (2013). Tunneling and the decision to go private: Evidence from Hong Kong. *Pacific-Basin Finance Journal, 22*, 50–68.

Engel, E., Hayes, R. M., & Wang, X. (2007). The Sarbanes-Oxley Act and firms' going-private decisions. *Journal of Accounting and Economics, 44*, 116–145.

Geranio, M., & Zanotti, G. (2012). Equity markets do not fit all: An analysis of public-to-private deals in Continental Europe. *European Financial Management, 18*(5), 867–895.

Halpern, P., Kieschnick, R. L., & Rotenberg, W. (1999). On the heterogeneity of leveraged going private transactions. *The Review of Financial Studies, 12*(2), 281–309.

Jensen, M. C. (1986). Agency costs of free cash flow, corporate finance, and takeovers. *The American Economic Review, 76*(2), 323–329.

Jensen, M. C. (1989). Eclipse of the public corporation. *Harvard Business Review, 67*(5), 61–37.
Kashefi Pour, E., & Lasfer, M. (2013). Why do companies delist voluntarily from the stock market? *Journal of Banking & Finance, 37*(12), 4850–4860.
Kieschnick, R. L. (1998). Free cash flow and stockholder gains in going private transactions revisited. *Journal of Business Finance and Accounting, 25*(1&2), 187–202.
Kim, W. S., & Lyn, E. O. (1991). Going private: Corporate restructuring under information asymmetry and agency problems. *Journal of Business Finance and Accounting, 18*, 637–648.
Krigman, L., Shaw, W. H., & Womack, K. L. (2001). Why do firms switch underwriters? *Journal of Financial Economics, 60*(2–3), 245–284.
Lehn, K., & Poulsen, A. (1989). Free cash flow and stockholder gains in going private transactions. *The Journal of Finance, 44*(3), 771–787.
Leuz, C., Triantis, A., & Wang, T. Y. (2008). Why do firms go dark? Causes and economic consequences of voluntary SEC deregistrations. *Journal of Accounting and Economics, 45*(2), 181–208.
Liu, S., Stowe, J. D., & Hung, K. (2012). Why US firms delist from the Tokyo stock exchange: An empirical analysis. *International Review of Economics & Finance, 24*, 62–70.
Macey, J., O'Hara, M., & Pompilio, D. (2008). Down and out in the stock market: The law and economics of the delisting process. *The Journal of Law and Economics, 51*(4), 683–713.
Marosi, A., & Massoud, N. (2007). Why do firms go dark? *Journal of Financial and Quantitative Analysis, 42*(2), 421–442.
Martinez, I., & Serve, S. (2011). The delisting decision: The case of buyout offer with squeeze-out (BOSO). *International Review of Law and Economics, 31*(4), 228–239.
Martinez, I., & Serve, S. (2017). Reasons for delisting and consequences: A literature review and research agenda. *Journal of Economic Surveys, 31*(3), 733–770.
Mehran, H., & Peristiani, S. (2010). Financial visibility and the decision to go private. *The Review of Financial Studies, 23*(2), 519–547.
Opler, T., & Titman, S. (1993). The determinants of leveraged buyout activity: Free cash flow vs. financial distress costs. *The Journal of Finance, 48*(5), 1985–1999.
Pagano, M., Panetta, F., & Zingales, L. (1998). Why do companies go public? An empirical analysis. *The Journal of Finance, 53*(1), 27–64.
Renneboog, L., Simons, T., & Wright, M. (2007). Why do public firms go private in the UK? The impact of private equity investors, incentive realignment and undervaluation. *Journal of Corporate Finance, 13*, 591–628.
Ritter, R. J. (1987). The costs of going public. *Journal of Financial Economics, 19*, 269–281.

Sanger, G. C., & Peterson, J. D. (1990). An empirical analysis of common stock delistings. *Journal of Financial and Quantitative Analysis, 25*(2), 261–272.

Shah, S., & Thakor, A. V. (1988). Private versus public ownership: Investment, ownership distribution, and optimality. *The Journal of Finance, 43*(1), 41–59.

Thomsen, S., & Vinten, F. (2014). Delistings and the costs of governance: A study of European stock exchanges 1996–2004. *Journal of Management & Governance, 18*(3), 793–833.

Weir, C., & Wright, M. (2006). Governance and takeovers: Are public-to-private transactions different from traditional acquisitions of listed corporations? *Accounting and Business Research, 36*(4), 289–307.

Weir, C., Laing, D., & Wright, W. (2005). Incentive effects, monitoring mechanisms and the market for corporate control: An analysis of the factors affecting public to private transactions in the UK. *Journal of Business Finance and Accounting, 32*(5), 909–943.

Index[1]

[1] Note: Page numbers followed by 'n' refer to notes.

B. Fidanza et al., *The Decision to Delist from the Stock Market*,
https://doi.org/10.1007/978-3-319-95049-5

The manufacturer's authorised representative in the EU is Springer Nature Customer Service Centre GmbH, Europaplatz 3, 69115 Heidelberg, Germany. If you have any concerns regarding our products, please contact ProductSafety@springernature.com

Printed and bound by CPI Group (UK) Ltd, Croydon, CR0 4YY

30/09/2026

02225653-0001